D1624260

MADE TO CHANGE THE WORLD

MADE TO CHANGE THE WORLD

How Ordinary People Are Called To Do Extraordinary Work, The Story of PROJECT 615

DEREK EVANS

Foreword by Mike Fisher,
Former captain of the Nashville Predators

Post Hill
PRESS

A POST HILL PRESS BOOK

Made to Change the World:
How Ordinary People Are Called To Do Extraordinary Work,
The Story of Project 615
© 2019 by Derek Evans
All Rights Reserved

ISBN: 978-1-64293-141-9
ISBN (eBook): 978-1-64293-142-6

Cover design by Derik Hobbs
Interior design and composition by Greg Johnson, Textbook Perfect

Post Hill Press
New York • Nashville
posthillpress.com

Published in the United States of America

Glory to God—Thank you for this journey.

To my parents, Debbie and Tracy—
You have showed me how to love well.

To my brother and sister, Trevor and Erin—
Thank you for your support and encouragement over the years.
You all mean the world to me.

To my beautiful wife, Mary—
I love you.

To my business partner and brother from another mother,
Matt Blinco—None of this would have been possible
without your patience, creativity, and strength.

To my niece, Nova, and nephews, Bentley and Joshua—
Remember, you are made to change the world.

CONTENTS

FOREWORD

If you live in Nashville it's a pretty safe bet you've heard of Project 615. Maybe you've been to Nashvember or the Nash Spring Bash, their annual outdoor fundraising events that bring together thousands of people for a fun day of live music and gourmet food trucks. Maybe you've seen Dolly, their vintage 1978 VW bus, driving around the streets of the city while they record live acoustic sessions with local bands and artists. Or maybe you've been to one of their retail stores, in West Nashville or Fatherland, and bought one of their cool hand-printed graphic tees. Even if you've never been to Nashville, there's a good chance you've seen their most iconic T-shirt, "Spread Love, It's the Nashville Way," worn by celebrities like Miley Cyrus, Lady Gaga, and my wife, Carrie Underwood.

But what a lot of people might not know is that since the company was founded in 2010, they have donated over half a million dollars from the profits of their T-shirt sales to at least twenty different world-changing organizations and employed over fifty people recovering from homelessness and addiction. Not bad for a couple of college buddies who started printing T-shirts out of the basement of an abandoned church.

I first met Project 615 cofounder Derek Evans in 2018 when he approached the team about partnering on a T-shirt design to raise money for the Predators Foundation, which works to improve the lives of youths and their families in Middle Tennessee. He came to us with the idea of releasing a limited-edition tee with the phrase "Unfinished Business"—a nod to my return to the team that season—that would be sold exclusively during the playoffs with 100 percent of the profits going to the foundation. Like most people in Middle Tennessee, I was aware of Project 615, but that is when I learned that they were more than just a cool local T-shirt brand. They are a company whose business model is built on a foundation of serving others and affecting change in the world through their products and company practices.

My own journey of service began when I was drafted to play for the Ottawa Senators at nineteen years old. At the time, I was a young kid trying to find my way and figure out who I was as a person and in my faith. I knew I had a gift that God had given to me and I wanted to use it to impact the world in a positive way, not just on the ice but off it. It took a few years for me to figure out what that looked like, but fortunately I was surrounded by a lot of good people in the Senators organization—from leadership to the players—who were doing so much for the community. It

Derek Evans (left), Mike Fisher (center, #12) and the Project 615 team.

inspired me to begin using the abilities and talent that I've been blessed with to help other people. I got involved with the team's foundation and began working with local children's charities. Once I started using my gifts and the platform that I had as an NHL player to make a difference in the world, I began to feel that I was finally on a path to fulfilling my purpose in life.

But it wasn't until years later that I truly understood the connection between my faith and the work I was doing. In 2014, Carrie and I traveled to Haiti on a mission trip with our church and Danita's Children, an incredible organization that provides education, pediatric medical and dental care, and homes to vulnerable and impoverished Haitian children and families. Over the next few days, we toured the Children's Center, where

Carrie helped out in the dental clinic; we spent time with the kids, playing basketball and soccer; and we visited the village to surprise families with gifts of food and supplies. The trip was transformative, but not for the reason I would have thought going in. I don't know if it's how we are inherently as people, but going into a mission trip like that, your mindset is that you're going down there to make a difference in *their* lives. Then you meet the children, you fall in love with them, and by the end of the experience you realize that they have done so much more for you than you could ever do for them. I was in my mid-thirties and that was one of the first times I'd gone on a mission trip. I realized: I have been missing out on so much joy and fulfillment in my life that comes from having experiences like this.

Our pastor was on the trip as well, and at one point he quoted a verse from James 1:27 that made me look at my faith in a whole new light: "Religion that God our father accepts as pure and faultless is this: to look after orphans or widows in their distress and to keep oneself from being polluted by the world." I was familiar with this scripture, and it had always stood out to me, but in the context of that experience he really made it come to life in a profound way. I realized that an essential component of faith is helping others in the name of Christ—and it's as simple as just doing your part to serve others.

I'm now on the board for Danita's Children, and for the past couple of years Carrie and I have hosted benefits to raise money to support the work that they're doing in Haiti. We both have a passion for this charity—and, obviously, people love to come see my wife sing—so it's a perfect blend. We each have our own organizations and projects that we support individually, but for us to have experienced the trip to Haiti together and then to be able to support Danita's as a married couple has been really special and meaningful for us.

You don't have to be an NHL athlete or a country music star to have an impact on the world. It doesn't matter how much money you make or how famous you are, we all have the capacity to affect powerful change in the world. I know a lot of people think that their impact won't be enough, but you just have to start by asking yourself, "What can I do to help?" That's essentially what the guys at Project 615 did. They saw a need and used their God-given talents to find a way to change the world, and they have touched thousands of lives along the way. That is what God can do if you take that step and commit to making a difference. You never know what can come of it.

We all have something inside us that brings value to the world. It's a matter of doing something positive with what we're given. Because everyone matters, and if we're all working together we have the potential to change lives and leave the world a better place than we found it.

—MIKE FISHER, *former Captain of the Nashville Predators*

CHAPTER 1

Love Your Neighbor

Truly I tell you, whatever you did for one of the least of these brothers and sisters of mine, you did for Me.

—JESUS (MATTHEW 25:40)

One cold, gray Tuesday evening in November, I found myself standing under the Jefferson Street Bridge in downtown Nashville serving dinner to hundreds of the city's homeless. I didn't want to be there. I was a college-educated, able-bodied white male in America who was still somehow one unemployment check away from being out on the street myself. The irony of serving a hot meal to the homeless when I could barely afford to feed myself was not lost on me. It was a point in my life where I felt I had sunk as low as I possibly could, and truthfully it's hard to feel compassion for others when you're busy feeling sorry for yourself. I had no idea then, but this experience would not only change my understanding of home-lessness—it would set me on course to my own salvation.

It's crazy how you can know with absolute certainty that you are on the wrong path, but still blindly follow it because stepping out into uncharted territory is too scary to contem-plate. Three months earlier, I was working an eight-to-five job for a general contractor in my hometown of Indianapolis and had just been given a promotion. I had a good job, a great salary, and my own office. At the age of twenty-four, my life ticked all the boxes for where I thought I should be. But, in truth, I was just going through the motions. It was like I was walking around in shoes that were two sizes too small, but everybody kept tell-ing me how great they looked, so I just kept putting one foot in front of the other. Deep down, I knew I was living a life that didn't fit. I had a yearning for something greater than the path laid out before me, but no idea how to escape the pressure to conform to what was expected of me.

When you grow up in a blue-collar community, the Ameri-can Dream is to land a good job with a steady income and stay there for the next forty years. Both my parents worked the same jobs their entire adult lives to put food on the table for their three children. My dad worked nights managing the boiler room at St. Francis Hospital, on the south side of Indianapolis.

He was a third-shift guy his whole life, so when we were getting home from school, he'd be just waking up and getting ready to go to work. My mother was the backbone of our family. She was the oldest of three sibling, so taking care of everyone around her came as naturally to her as breathing. When she wasn't in the kitchen cooking for me and my brother and sister or driving us back and forth to church youth groups and our various sports activities, she was helping my dad make ends meet by working a full-time job as a secretary. On the rare occasion we went out to eat as a family, we knew it was a payday.

I don't remember my parents ever taking a day off from work my entire childhood, but I was still acutely aware growing up that, no matter how hard they worked, we still didn't have enough. One of my earliest memories is of being at the checkout of our local supermarket and my mom carefully counting out pennies, nickels, and dimes from her purse to pay the cashier for our weekly grocery shop. When she had handed over the last of our coins to the lady with big, frizzy red hair standing on the other side of our small pile of groceries, it was clear even to me that this was all the money we had. The lady scowled at us over her dime-store readers and then announced—in a tone that made my mom straighten her back—we were *still* a couple of dollars short. What sticks with me most about that moment is the look on my mother's face as she pleaded with that woman for a little bit of grace. I was only four years old, but I knew what sadness looked like. I didn't know the words, but I also knew what pride and shame and desperation looked like. I remember looking up at this woman who seemed to have the power to decide whether or not we would have enough to eat that week, and the expression on her face was anything but kind.

If the bottom hadn't fallen out of the construction industry in 2008, I'd probably still be sitting behind a desk in Indianapolis. For years, I had been daydreaming about moving to another city and starting my own business, but I had learned from experience to keep those fantasies to myself. Whenever I shared one of my ideas with friends or my family I was always met with the same blank expression. For as long as I could remember, I had been marching to a different beat than everyone around me and by then, I was resigned to the idea that it was *me* who was out of step.

Then, one sunny August afternoon, a few months after I had been given the promotion I thought I wanted, my boss walked into my office and told me the company was going under. He shook my hand, thanked me for all my hard work, and handed me a severance check for $1,000. I knew that I should have been devastated—or, at the very least, seriously concerned about my immediate financial security—but all I could feel in that moment was this huge sense of relief. I didn't have any idea what I wanted to do with my life, but I knew for damn sure that I didn't want to spend it sitting in that office.

My first thought was: *I'm going to Nashville.* A college buddy of mine had moved down there to be with his girlfriend, who was working for the Country Music Hall of Fame. It was just a four-and-a-half-hour drive from Indianapolis, so I had gone down to visit him a couple of times in the last year and had fallen in love with the city. I had expected Nashville to be this honky-tonk town populated by cowboy-boot-wearing good ol' boys, but it turned out to be a vibrant city full of musicians, artists, athletes, and entrepreneurs looking to make their mark on the world. It struck me as this place where people from all walks of life come to pursue their dreams. I wasn't sure what dream I was chasing or what I would do for work when I got there, but I figured nothing could feel worse than slowly suffocating behind a desk in Indiana.

That same day, I drove to my parents' house and announced, "I'm moving to Nashville and I'm going to start a T-shirt company."

Not surprisingly, their reaction was, "Are you insane? What do you know about selling T-shirts, much less starting a business?" Like any typical twenty-something who experiences pushback from his parents after presenting his questionable life plan, their doubt became fuel for the fire in my belly—even though I was only about 70 percent sure I would prove them wrong.

Their skepticism was actually pretty understandable. I had absolutely no idea how to go about starting a business. I had a degree in broadcast journalism but had abandoned that career path after a brief stint working for the ESPN affiliate in Indianapolis. It was a dream internship, but it became clear to me when Kobe Bryant scored eighty-one points against the Toronto Raptors that broadcast journalism wasn't what I wanted to do with my life. I had gone into work that next morning and everyone in the office was going crazy—after all, it was the second most prolific single-game scoring performance in NBA history. I remember looking around at the frenzy of activity and feeling like I just didn't care the way everyone else did. I realized that I loved sports, but I didn't want to spend my life talking about sports stats. I remember at that moment thinking: *I want to do work that matters and make a real difference in people's lives.*

So, full of the idealism of a kid fresh out of college, I quit that internship and went to work for a Christian summer camp in Michigan and then landed in a leadership role at the YMCA in Indianapolis. I didn't yet know what my purpose was, but I figured working with kids was a good place to start. I spent the next couple of years subsisting on a nonprofit salary, while my college buddies worked their way up the corporate ladder. After a while, I began to feel like I was getting left behind. So I stopped listening to that voice inside that was telling me to find meaning in my work and took a job in construction management. I hated the job, but loved the salary and resigned myself to settling into a nice, comfortable rut.

I am a person of faith. I believe that there are moments in life where opportunities appear disguised as obstacles, but if we seize those moments and take that leap into the great unknown, we open ourselves to outcomes we never imagined possible. When my boss walked into my office that day and told me he was letting me go, it felt like a deeply spiritual moment where God was telling me, "This is not where you belong. Go now, and find your true path." It was the sign I had been waiting for and, quite possibly, the last chance I would have to figure out my life on my own terms.

My college buddy hooked me up with a friend of his who was looking to rent a room in his apartment in Antioch: a diverse, low-income neighborhood on the south side of Nashville that was still affordable at the time because of its reputation for crime and urban blight. Six days later, I had packed up my belongings and was in my car heading for what I hoped would be a fresh start in Nashville. I didn't have a plan but I figured I would give myself a year to figure it out. The thing about faith is that it requires you to believe even in the face of overwhelming doubt. And in the year to come, my faith in myself and in the path that I had chosen would be tested over and over again.

I had left Indianapolis, in part, because it was just embarrassing to be in my hometown and not have my life figured out. It seemed like everyone around me knew what they wanted out of life and was taking steps to get there. In Nashville, I might fail but at least I would be just another face in the crowd. I just had no idea, until I found myself living in a city where I only knew one person, how lonely and isolating that could feel. I couldn't find work and the money I had from my severance check ran out almost immediately. Thankfully, unemployment benefits came into play. It wasn't much money, but it was a life raft that kept my head above water—though barely. Things went from desperate to dire when my car died on me. I was actually on my way back to Indianapolis for my college homecoming. I was about an hour out of Nashville when the transmission blew, and I had to get towed back to the city. I still owed thousands of dollars on the car and a new transmission would have cost thousands more, so getting it repaired or getting a new car was not an option.

I just kept thinking: *Why? Why is this happening to me?* I had no job and barely enough money coming in from unemployment to cover my rent, much less the loan I was now paying off for a car I no longer had. I couldn't even afford Internet access, so I had to either scrounge up the cash for a taxi or rely on my roommate to drive me to the library so I could apply for jobs online. I felt like I was that four-year-old kid again, hoping for a little bit of mercy from a world that seemed to have none to give. Self-pity is an insidious creature. It seeps in through the dark corners of your psyche and wraps its oily tentacles around your soul until its grip is so tight you feel like you can barely breathe. It was in this moment of emotional, spiritual, and financial crisis that I found hope and inspiration in the most unlikely of places.

It probably won't surprise anyone when I confess, at this point, that I did not go down to the bridge that day out of any altruistic desire to help my fellow man. The truth is I was there because a pretty girl had invited me, and (being broke and unemployed) I had nothing better to do anyway. We had met at Kairos, a young adult ministry in Nashville that attracted a lot of musicians, artists, and hipster types. I don't know what I was expecting when she said that she and a few friends from Kairos were going down to feed the homeless under the Jefferson Street Bridge and asked if I wanted to join them. I had traveled over that deserted patch of trash-strewn gravel at least a dozen times in the past few months without giving it so much as a second glance. I was about to learn, however, that once a week, rain or shine, this otherwise desolate location came alive with the sound of gospel music as hundreds of Nashville's most marginalized and needy residents gathered for what I can only describe as part block party, part mass feeding, part evangelical church service.

I would learn later that the Bridge Ministry was born in 2004, when founder Candy Christmas, a former Southern gospel music star, was inspired by her local pastor to begin driving down to the Jefferson Street Bridge with a big pot of homemade jambalaya to feed a group of homeless people out of the back of her car. Four years later, it had grown into a well-oiled operation with mobile kitchens capable of preparing and distributing hot meals for hundreds of people. There were trucks loaded with clothing, coats, shoes, tents, sleeping bags, toiletries, and dry goods to be distributed at the end of the evening. Dozens of volunteers were stationed at long folding tables, serving hot dogs, baked beans, macaroni, chips, and bottles of cold water to the hundreds of hungry people who had been lining up for hours waiting for what was most likely their first meal of the day.

Directly under the bridge was a makeshift stage area, set up with lights and sound equipment, where veteran singers and musicians from Nashville's gospel music scene were performing "Amazing Grace" before a crowd of people sitting shoulder to shoulder in rows of plastic folding chairs. Some of the older homeless were standing and singing along, cheering and praising God. I saw one woman who had tears streaming down her face as she sang along—whether they were tears of joy or sorrow, I couldn't say.

As a volunteer, I was not only serving food but also interacting with the people who had come to be fed. I shook hands and listened to their stories. It was a little nerve-racking at first, because you weren't sure what was going to happen from one moment to the next. Sure, there were the people who had come for a hot meal, a little compassion, and some basic supplies, but there was also the guy talking to himself ten feet from where I was standing, who I was pretty sure was high on crack.

There were people of all ages and ethnicities. Some were struggling with addiction or mental illness, or both. Some were living on the streets, some in shelters or out of their cars. Some were drunk or high, and causing a scene. Some people weren't talking or eating, but just sat quietly smoking cigarettes and staring off into space. Most of them had nothing in common but the defining need to rely on the kindness of strangers to make it through to the next day. It was loud and messy and chaotic, but also profoundly beautiful and joyous.

As the sky grew darker, the sound of gospel music gave way to the soothing tone of a pastor's sermon. Volunteers from the Bridge Ministry had packed away the last of the food and were now mixed in among the crowd, talking to and praying with the homeless—the differences between them blurring in the fading evening light of early winter. I was standing there, still ruminating over my own woe-is-me situation, when the girl I had followed down to the bridge tapped me on the shoulder. She said she and her friends were going to pray with the some of the homeless and asked if I wanted to come.

We started talking to this one guy, an older white man with long, stringy, unwashed hair who had been sitting on his own for most of the night. I didn't want to talk to this guy or pray with him. I was pretty sure he was drunk because I could smell the alcohol on his breath. He told us he was in need of strength and guidance, so we gathered around him and began to pray. I remember huddling up, praying over this man and suddenly realizing with humbling clarity that there was no difference between us. I may have had a roof over my head, but if things kept going in the direction they were going, it could easily be me coming down to the bridge in need of a hot meal.

There but for the grace of God...

It was like the ground shifted under my feet and the door to my compassion swung wide open. As I looked down at the weather-beaten face of that homeless man, I couldn't help but think of my maternal grandfather, Robert Lunn. Whatever understanding I had at that point of homelessness had been shaped by his stories of the years he had spent as a young man living on the streets. He had grown up on a farm in the rural South, raised by a mother who had seven other children at her hip and a father who got violent when he was drunk, which was often. At the age of thirteen, he ran away from home with nothing but the shirt on his back and the certainty that any kind of life was better than waiting around for another beating from his dad. He spent the next few years hoboing around the country, moving south when the weather got cold and taking odd jobs in exchange for food and lodging. When he was old enough to enlist in the army, he quit that life and was shipped off to fight in Korea.

As a child, I was fascinated by my grandpa's stories. I used to envision this period of his life as a sepia-toned montage of his most romantic tales: my grandpa as a rakish, rail-thin boy hopping freight trains from state to state; drinking the alcohol out of shaving cream to catch a buzz because he had no money for real whiskey; stealing a car with a couple of buddies and driving it to San Francisco, where they ended up being chased by the police over the Golden Gate Bridge; working twelve hours a day as pin boy at a bowling alley in exchange for a decent night's sleep on a cot behind the lanes; enlisting in the army at seventeen so he could have three square meals a day, a decent pair of boots on his feet, and a place to rest his head at night.

After the war, he settled in Indianapolis, where he met and fell in love with my grandmother, who was sixteen and working at the local movie theater. She was already pregnant with my mother when they got married and he spent the next thirty years working as a janitor at the local elementary school and raising their three children.

Growing up, Grandpa always called himself a hobo—even though, by the time I was born, that part of his life must have been a distant memory. He kept his home so spotlessly clean, you could practically eat off the floor. The smell of clean laundry always hung in the air. I remember him telling me that living on the streets made him that way. The mark of homelessness was indelible. It never left him. It was like an oily stain under his

Robert Lunn, grandfather to Derek, in Korea.

fingernails that he could never erase, no matter how hard he scrubbed.

My grandpa and I had a special bond. He was the kind of guy who went to church three times a week, but could also enjoy a beer with the pastor after the service. He was a rebel whose moral compass pointed true north. He was born in an era when Jim Crow laws were still very much in effect in the deep South, but when it came to people he was totally color-blind—his best friend was a fellow janitor whose skin just happened to be black. He was a man who lived by the principle of compassion and love for his fellow man.

Grandpa passed away in 2003, five years before I moved to Nashville, but he remains a powerfully inspirational influence in my life. He appears in my dreams often. I can still smell him and hear his laughter. I would only learn, years later, that the farm he grew up on was in Dickson County, Tennessee, just a half-hour outside Nashville. I've always wondered if the spiritual pull that brought me to Nashville had something to do with the fact that Robert Lunn's family had been born and died in Dickson, going back at least five generations.

As I stood under the Jefferson Street Bridge that night, praying over a homeless man I did not know and would never see again, I thought about my grandpa as a boy living on the street and the impact that had on the man he would become. I thought about this homeless man and wondered what happened in his life that had brought him to this place. I thought about what a little bit of compassion can do for a person's soul.

It would still be another two years before I found my way to Project 615, but a seed was planted in my heart that night that would ultimately grow into a mission. Today, the mission of my life and the mission of my business are one and the same, and that is to love my neighbor. This is the principal my grandfather lived by and it's at the core of everything I do both personally and professionally. Not long ago, I had a dream that I saw my grandpa on the street in Nashville. He walked up to me, put his hand on my shoulder and told me he was proud of me.

CHAPTER 2

The City of Dreams

"Having dreams is what makes life tolerable."

—FROM the movie *Rudy*

One of the coolest things about arriving at a point in life where you're living the dream you've worked so hard to turn into a reality is that you find yourself running into versions of your younger self and you are able to pass on a little bit of the wisdom you've accumulated along the way. Not long ago, I stopped into a coffee shop on my way to work and noticed the guy behind the counter was wearing a Project 615 T-shirt. We struck up a conversation and I was surprised by how much he actually knew about our business and the outreach we do with the homeless community in Nashville.

He had graduated from the University of Arizona, where he was a Division I swimmer, and was now back home in Nashville working at a coffee shop and wondering what to do with the rest of his life. He had just been promoted to shift manager, but he confided to me that what he really wanted to do was be a coach and start a youth swim club. He had a dream he wanted to follow, but the barriers seemed insurmountable. A huge part of him felt like maybe he should just be a coffee shop manager and pay his bills and student loans.

I knew exactly how he felt. He was a young guy, maybe twenty-two or twenty-three. I was about his age when I started the journey that would lead me to the creation of Project 615— and it wasn't exactly a straight line from point A to point B. The road from unemployed to entrepreneur is winding and filled with steep climbs and unexpected pitfalls. There were times I questioned my own sanity for banking my future on the crazy idea that a T-shirt company could actually make a difference in other people's lives. I knew all too well what it was like to feel like you have to choose between following a passion and paying your rent. I felt an obligation to pour into this guy and began to share my story with him.

I told him that, if I had learned anything in the ten years since I packed up my car and moved to Nashville with the dream of finding my purpose, it's that you don't have to go down a traditional path to be successful in life. We are each born with a desire to do something great. By embracing our natural gifts and talents, we give purpose to our actions and meaning to our lives. When we are driven by passion, our potential becomes boundless. Whether your calling is to be a swim coach and impact the lives of kids in your community or to build a socially responsible business, you must take the leap of faith required to follow that path, because that is how our dreams become our reality.

Nine months after moving to Nashville, the path ahead of me was no clearer than it had been when I left Indiana. I had applied for hundreds of jobs and had nothing to show for it. I got called in for an interview at the YMCA in Nashville. I did not get the position. I got called in to interview for an entry-level management position at Dollar General headquarters in Good-lettsville, just north of the city. I didn't get that job either. That was it. For the most part, I'd send off my résumé and never hear back. I had no income and was barely able to cover rent with my meager unemployment check. I was so desperate (and broke), I tried calling the Department of Human Services to apply for food stamps. Having to make that call was probably the most humiliating moment of my life—and the worst part was that I got turned down because I actually made too much income through my unemployment benefits to qualify for food stamps. I remember hanging up the phone and feeling sick to my stomach. I felt like I was falling apart. I kept thinking, "How have I fallen this far? Why, God? Why is this happening to me? What are you teaching me?"

I was getting by doing odd jobs for people on Craigslist. I had a friend who worked for a market research company who would hook me up, from time to time, with a gig where they paid you with a forty-dollar Visa gift card to hang out for a couple of hours and talk about certain products. Anything I owned that had value (which wasn't much) went up on Craigslist whenever I needed money for food or didn't have enough to make rent. I was hustling all these side gigs with the hope that my dream of building something on my own that gave meaning to my life would be attainable soon.

Music has always been a powerful source of creative inspiration for me. For my high school graduation, I was given money for college expenses. I bought turntables instead. I taught myself how to spin and my investment paid off when I started DJing for side money in college. Since I wasn't having any luck sending my résumé out in pursuit of a corporate gig, I started DJing again for fraternity and sorority parties in Nashville. It was a fun way to scratch up some extra cash, and I felt an affinity with my artist and musician friends. They were just as broke as I was, but they were living their dreams and that's what I was trying to do. It's why I had come to Nashville in the first place. Being around that kind of energy was not only validating, it was electrifying. I was having a blast playing music and connecting with other young people in the city. Then some guy at a frat party offered me a line of cocaine to play his favorite song. I politely declined, but it was like a fog had lifted. I suddenly realized that, as much as I loved the creative outlet that being DJ gave me, spinning tracks for college students was not my calling.

My roommate had been pretty cool with me when I was late with the rent but, by that point, it was happening more regularly than either one of us was comfortable with. He was working a nine-to-five job as a claims associate for State Farm and I knew I had exhausted his patience when he mentioned they had an opening in his department and said he could get me the job if I wanted it. The State Farm Operations Center was in Murfreesboro, about a forty-five-minute commute each way from Nashville, and I was still without a car, but he had a carpool going with some of the guys he worked with and generously offered to let me ride with them. It was humbling because he and I were peers. I was seeing all these things work out for him in his life. He owned the condo we were living in. He had a good job with a steady income. He wasn't paying off a car that had died on him a year ago. And here I was, basically falling apart right in front of him under his roof. The last thing I wanted was for someone to have to come in and rescue me, but the choice was pretty simple: keep hustling and scraping together just enough each month to survive, or swallow my pride and thank him for hooking me up with both a job and ride to work.

The job at State Farm was essentially a paid trial period, where you prepared to take their Employment Selection Test. Sitting behind a desk in a cubicle wasn't exactly living my dream, but I quickly fell back into the mindset I had before I got laid off in Indiana: This isn't my passion, but it's a real job with a real future, and an even more real paycheck. For the first time in months, I could pay my rent on time, buy groceries, and even set a little aside towards getting a new car. Best of all, I was able to tell people that I had a job so I didn't feel like a failure. Things were finally looking up.

I was hired with a team of seven other people and we spent our days studying for the test and sitting in on HR workshops that covered everything from sexual harassment in the workplace to dress code and customer service. I was bored out of my mind and, to pass the time, I fell into the role of class clown. Instead of studying, I was sending funny YouTube videos to the other people on my team. I figured I was a reasonably intelligent guy. I had a college education. How hard could it be to pass this test? Meanwhile, I was still fantasizing about finding a way to get my own business off the ground, so I could step off the corporate hamster wheel and make a living doing something I was passionate about.

I wasn't sure I believed in myself, but fortunately, I had someone in my life who did. I first met Matt Blinco at a St. Patrick's Day party in Rushville, Indiana, back when I was still trying to convince myself I was happy working for a general contractor. We knew each other peripherally because we were both in the same fraternity in college, but he was a couple of years younger and still finishing up his senior year. At the time, I was toying with the idea of writing a book about high school basketball in Indiana. I would tell people about it, and every single time, I got the same reaction: "Don't you already have a good job?"

Matt was probably the hundredth person I shared it with, and he looked at me and said with earnest and infectious enthusiasm, "That's an amazing idea!" He was the first person I met post-college who actually understood where I was coming from.

A handful of months after that conversation, I made a trip back to my alma mater, Anderson University in Indiana, to visit some fraternity buddies who hadn't graduated yet. I was supposed to stay the night with a friend, but he ended up bailing on me to hang out with his girlfriend. By default, I wound up crashing on Matt's couch. That was the first of many nights where we laughed and brainstormed and realized that we shared the same creative drive and longing to build something that mattered. That moment of connection opened a door for a brotherly bond and began a two-year-long conversation where we were passionately trying coming up with ideas we could work on together. We shared the same irreverent sense of humor, so we would have had all these late-night conversations where we talked about moving to Los Angeles to write comedy or starting some kind of business together.

Matt was four years younger and still transitioning from college student to working adult, so in the beginning, I was kind of like a big brother to him. I remember, a year after he graduated, he still had this college-guy outgoing message on his voicemail, so I gently pointed out that, if we were going to start a business together, "Hey. What's up? You know what to do," might not project the most professional tone. Two years later, the friendship had grown from me being an older brother/ mentor to an equal partnership where we were working toward achieving the same dreams and goals.

The idea behind starting a T-shirt company was born out of a blog called *Life With Us Three* that I had started with a couple of buddies from the same fraternity, where we took turns writing short stories that had a comedy element as a way to stay in touch after college. Matt wasn't one of the original "Three," but he would regularly contribute content as a guest blogger. One of our catchphrases was "What Up, Maine" (like, "What up, man?" but pronounced like the state). That led the four of us to begin hashing over the idea of taking that phrase and making it into a T-shirt that we could sell to people from Maine. Matt had studied graphic design in college, so he created a cool graphic for the tee that we tried to sell on Craigslist in Maine. I don't think we sold a single shirt.

Despite our admittedly less-than-impressive entrepreneurial debut, I instinctively knew we were onto something. It was one of those things where the other two guys involved weren't as motivated or interested, but for Matt and me, the experience kicked open the door to a creative flow that felt like a lifeline. We started having all these sidebar conversations where we were coming up with all kinds of ideas for graphic T-shirts with a humorous edge. By the time I decided to move to Nashville, I had locked onto it as a legitimate idea I could sell to my parents as a way of supporting myself.

Nine months later, I was sitting behind a desk in Murfeesboro, Tennessee, once again trying to fit my square peg into a very round, very corporate hole. Matt had done an internship in Nashville the year before and was hoping to eventually move back one day, but the only job he could get out of college was for a graphic design firm in Owensboro, Kentucky. He was the kind of guy who was always up for a road trip, so he would drive down to visit me in Nashville and we would have epic brainstorming sessions for how we could realize our dream of getting our own business off the ground. We'd stay up into the wee hours of the night, drinking cheap beer, eating cheap wings, watching sports, and playing video games, as we spitballed silly phrases back and forth that we could turn into marketable T-shirt designs.

Matt had designed shirts in college as a side gig and I had enough work experience by then to handle marketing and sales, so launching a T-shirt business seemed like a no-brainer. We thought we were pretty funny guys, so the concept was to just design silly shirts that made people smile and position ourselves as an apparel brand that met all your ironic T-shirt needs. Now we just needed a name. Initially, we wanted it to have a Christian element, so we talked about naming the company Sea Walk Tees (as a nod to the miracle of Jesus walking on water). I don't remember why we didn't go with that name—probably just because it was so esoteric that nobody would get the reference. In the end, we landed on Huggable Tees—which, for some reason, we thought would convey our sense of humor. (Technically speaking, we didn't have a single sale with Huggable Tees, although, to this day, we're pretty sure we may have sold a few of our designs. Unfortunately, because we launched a website that linked to Matt's boss at the time, who ran and developed websites, the money would have gone into his bank account and we never saw a penny.)

Even though at that point, I was still thinking of the business as a side hustle, I was so preoccupied with getting the website for Huggable Tees set up that my heart and mind were definitely not with State Farm. When they were teaching us all the policy stuff that was going to be on the Employment Selection Test, I was so focused on coming up with clever T-shirt ideas that I wasn't absorbing any of it. About six weeks into our training, my team was given the test. It was a hundred questions and they gave you three chances to pass, but really, it was so straightforward that there were people working there with barely more than an eighth-grade education who passed it the first time. I thought I could fake my way through it. It turned out I couldn't.

Most of the people on my team passed the first time. I failed miserably. The next month, I had to take it again and, this time, I actually studied. "No sweat, Derek," my teammates kept reassuring me. "You got this." When I failed the second time, they started to look at me a little differently. I could tell they were worried, but they still patted me on the back and said positive and encouraging things like, "Don't worry, you'll get it next time for sure," and "Third time's a charm!" By then, I was the only one left from my entire team who hadn't passed. The next month, I took the test again and failed for the third time—which pretty much never happens. I remember thinking, "You have got to be kidding me. I've taken this test three freakin' times and failed all three? What is going on?" Next thing I knew, I was back in my cubicle, where there was a box on my desk with all my stuff in it and a security guard waiting to escort me out of the building. That was utterly demoralizing.

I had thought I was at a point where I had finally picked myself up and life was starting to go my way but, once again, I'd fallen down. I had assumed I was going to be at State Farm for years, that I'd move up the ladder and eventually become a manager. Instead, I was back to being broke and collecting unemployment. It was worse than when I got laid off back in Indianapolis. Way worse. It was even more devastating than when I got denied for food stamps. This time the rejection felt like a gut punch. Looking back, I am able see it as a defining moment where God was leading me on a journey for greater things, but it definitely did not feel that way at the time. But once I stopped feeling sorry for myself, getting fired from State Farm ended up lighting a fire under me and fueled that desire to chase my dream. I could finally see with absolute clarity that starting my own business was a path I needed to follow, and not just part-time—because it was painfully clear that I wasn't cut out for a corporate job.

We weren't getting much traction with Huggable Tees, so in January 2010, Matt and I launched a new company: Cannonball Creative. Since we were 0 for 2 with our "shirt companies," we started thinking: What if we just designed for other people and other companies? We both had a passion for music, so why not create cool artwork, logos, and T-shirts for musicians and bands in Nashville? I started cold-calling screen print shops all over the country offering to create designs for them for ten dollars an hour. Within a couple of months, I had contacted just about every screen-printing company in America. A lot of them didn't have a designer on staff, so they took us up on our offer and we started to build a little side hustle as freelance designers. Matt would create the graphics and I would handle the accounts. What we really wanted was to develop our own brand, but at least we were in the game.

After years of struggling and searching, I was finally moving in the right direction. It felt like that moment in *Rudy* when, even after getting rejected from Notre Dame three times, he refuses to give up and finally gets in as a walk-on. Perseverance is a beautiful, magical gift. When I think back on this period of my journey and the triumph of turning rejection into fuel for the fire that was deep inside of me, I'm reminded of the opening verse in James 1:2 NIV, "Consider it pure joy when you go through trials and tribulations because it makes you stronger." In life, we can't always choose our path or control our circumstances, but we *can* choose to perceive adversity as opportunity, because those challenges and ordeals help us develop a deeper trust in ourselves and in God. Sometimes we need to be knocked off the ledge before we realize we can fly.

There was still a long road ahead before the work we were doing would crystalize into a vision for a philanthropic business, but this was the moment that I stopped trying to follow the herd and began to trust in myself and my own unique gifts and talents. It was a leap of faith that was truly terrifying, but there is so much beauty on the other side of that fear. We all have something in us that comes naturally and that's the thing we have to home in on. That's the energy and strength that will take our dreams to the next level. There's so much more to life if you simply follow your heart.

CHAPTER 3

Do Everything in Love

"Everybody can be great, because anybody can serve."

—DR. MARTIN LUTHER KING JR.

A couple of years ago, I was at a Titans game in downtown Nashville and I ran into a guy who had been on my team at State Farm. He was still working there, still sitting behind the same desk in the same cubicle, crunching insurance numbers and calling people about their car wrecks. When he asked what I had been up to since we last saw each other, I told him about Project 615. He looked genuinely impressed.

"Whoa, that's *your* company?" he said. "I remember you always talking about starting your own business, but I figured you were just daydreaming."

Then he hugged me and said, "Dude, you did it!"

It was like that final scene in *The Shawshank Redemption* where Red goes down to Zihuatanejo as a free man to reunite with Andy, who has escaped from prison.

When the vision behind Project 615 had first begun to take shape back in the summer of 2010, to quote Morgan Freeman's closing lines from the movie, I felt "the excitement only a free man can feel, a free man at the start of a long journey whose conclusion is uncertain." For months, Matt and I had been scrapping together a couple hundred bucks here and there through Cannonball Creative, designing T-shirts for screen-printing companies all over the country. It wasn't much of an income, but it was enough that I didn't have to take a minimum-wage job packing groceries or stacking boxes in the stock room at a sporting goods store. The goal was still to get our own brand off the ground, but for the first time in my life, I felt this sense of pride and fulfillment that can only come from truly working towards building something of your own.

I was still technically unemployed and had a lot of free time on my hands, so I began to think about ways we could evolve from two funny college buddies who design silly T-shirts into successful entrepreneurs. There was still something missing from what we were building, some integral piece I couldn't quite define that would not only set our brand apart but also give meaning to our work. I didn't know it then, but Matt and

I were about to embark on a life-changing trip that would radically redefine our concept of what our business could be and set us on course for a lifelong journey of helping others.

A couple of months earlier, I had mentioned to a friend that I had done a little bit of homeless outreach with the Bridge Ministry and she suggested that I sign up for a mission trip that Kairos was organizing to serve the homeless in Los Angeles. I had never been to California, so I was definitely intrigued. Unfortunately, I was also broke. The trip only cost $1,000, which covered airfare, meals, and accommodation for ten days, but at that point, I was lucky if I had $100 in the bank. When I found out Kairos would front the money for the trip and allow a year's grace to pay them back, I was like, "Heck, yeah. Sign me up." Eight weeks later, I was on a flight bound for La-La Land, where I would spend the next ten days doing outreach in Skid Row, home to one of the largest stable homeless populations in the country.

It had been a year since I had volunteered under the bridge and I felt like this trip could reignite that sense of purpose I felt that night. Or maybe I just wanted a cheap trip to Los Angeles. It's hard to say how much I was motivated by a will to help the homeless and how much by my own selfish desires. I had just come out of this dark period where I had spent four months cooped up in a cubicle at State Farm. I wanted to live a little and travel. The idea of a trip to Los Angeles (that I didn't have to pay for right away) seemed like just what I needed to clear the cobwebs and get my creative juices flowing again.

Coincidentally (or as part of God's plan for us), Matt had also been planning a mission trip to New Orleans the same week with his own church in Owensboro. When that trip fell through at the last minute, he asked if he could join our trip and a couple of weeks later drove down to Nashville so we could all fly into LAX as a group. There is no way of knowing if Matt and I would have gone on to become partners in some kind of successful enterprise if we hadn't been on this trip together. We were young and ambitious and that was certainly our intention. What I do know with absolute certainly is that being together in that place and in that moment in time would have an indelible impact on us both, and would alter the course of both our lives.

Kairos had organized the trip in partnership with Set Free Ministries, an evangelical church that ministers to the poor, drug addicts, the homeless, former gang members, bikers, and ex-felons. As part of our introduction to their faith-based homeless/addiction recovery program, they took us to visit their headquarters in Yucaipa, California, about an hour east of Los Angeles, where they have a ranch in the foothills of the San Bernardino Mountains dedicated to the rehabilitation of lost souls. Founded by survivors of addiction and homelessness, the goal of the Set Free Ranch (and the church in general) is to provide a safe place for a person who just got out of prison, has been living on the streets, or has been struggling with addiction to begin the process of rebuilding their lives. They've taken a lot of the recovery model from programs like Alcoholics Anonymous and Narcotics Anonymous and applied it to the larger issue of homelessness. They take away your phone, if you have one. You can't be in contact with anybody outside the ranch for ninety days because they truly want you to focus on the reset. They introduce you to God and the Christian faith. It's a rehab, but not the kind that celebrities go to. They operate with very little money, relying mostly on donations from people within the ministry and a handful of other churches who support their mission. At the ranch, they have a saying, "It's beans and rice and Jesus Christ." It's not Betty Ford, but for the one hundred men and forty women housed there, it's three square meals a day and a chance to regain their footing and turn their lives around. There are people who come through the program who truly change forever. There are people who never change. And there are people who fall down and pick themselves up a hundred times.

After ninety days at the ranch, Set Free will set you up in a halfway house where they provide a stable and sober living environment and help you find a steady job. It's an incremental recovery program designed to help those who have fallen the farthest get back up on their feet. One of the most transformational parts of the trip was the opportunity for fellowship when we gathered together at the halfway house in downtown LA and got to know some of the people who were coming up through the program. It was all these Hells Angels-looking biker guys, who were ex-cons or former homeless drug addicts but had reformed their lives and were now trying to rescue, save, serve, love on, and feed people in Skid Row.

Some of these men (and women) had been living on the streets or in prison for a decade or more, but now they had jobs as busboys and security guards. They had been in the program long enough that they had achieved some sobriety and were on the road to restoring their lives. These guys were our buddies for the week. They acted as our guides and bodyguards in Skid Row, and we were able to get to know them and hear their stories. It was so inspiring to hear what they had been through and how they had begun to pull their lives together. These people had emerged from the depths of darkness and despair with their souls intact and our time with them yielded some of the most beautiful and inspiring moments of that trip.

The beauty of the program is that all the pastors come from the streets. There are Set Free ministries all over the country and they are all run by people who have survived poverty, prison, homelessness, or addiction (often all four). They come into the program and change their lives. After a period of maturity, sobriety, trust, and accountability, Set Free raises them up to be pastors. And then they go and plant their own churches, where they continue the mission of helping others get off the streets. It's a beautiful concept. You take a guy who can really relate to the drug dealer, to the addict, to the biker, and to the ex-felon—he's able to speak their language and pull them up from the abyss because he's been to the bottom and knows exactly how hard it is to claw your way back up.

The ranch is where the lost can find a path to salvation and the halfway house is where they become accountable for their lives, but Skid Row is the pond where Set Free pastors and volunteers fish for those lost souls that can be saved. They go into Skid Row to feed these people and speak the truth to them. They love on them and let them know that, if they want a better life, they can come back to the ranch in Yucaipa to get clean and sober.

Our goal for this trip was simply to provide spiritually in the form of Bible study, fellowship, and prayer, and to provide physically in the form of food. There was a lot of hype about Skid Row in the weeks leading up to the trip, so we felt a fair amount of nervous anticipation going in—almost like going to a haunted house. Our team leaders kept telling us, "You are about to experience something crazy." We were all thinking: How crazy can it be? I had already dipped my toes in homeless outreach as a volunteer with the Bridge Ministry, so I was kind of feeling myself and thinking I could handle anything they threw at me. I was wrong.

Skid Row was unlike anything any of us had ever experienced. Estimates vary widely but at any given time, there are anywhere from two thousand to five thousand lost souls sleeping on the streets of this 0.4-square-mile, roughly fifty-city-block wasteland. It was like we had been transported to a third world country or some kind of dystopian nightmare. We were warned to stay together, to avoid eye contact, and look away if we got scared. It was me, ten young women, Matt, and one other guy—a baker's dozen of white, Christian twenty-somethings going into this no-man's-land where murderers, criminals, and drug addicts mixed with the mentally ill, disabled, and afflicted. What was there to be scared of, right? (Who am I kidding? Of course we were terrified. Skid Row is hell on Earth.)

The first thing that hits you is the smell. It's a mixture of weed, vomit, rotting garbage, feces, urine, and other bodily fluids baked by the mid-July California sun into a steamy, putrid stench that I can only describe as the smell of human misery and despair. There were people staring and mean-mugging us everywhere we went. We had to step over men and women who were sleeping on the sidewalk in rows, lined up one after another for block after block in makeshift tents or on cardboard mats. There were people literally going the bathroom on the street in front of us—I'm talking squatting down in broad daylight and relieving the contents of their bowels right onto the sidewalk. The porta-potties were the domain of prostitutes and addicts who used them to either shoot up drugs or to sell their bodies for money to buy drugs. We encountered people who must have been in their fifties or sixties, but who only had the verbal capacity of a six-year-old; people who were clearly mentally ill, threatening to kill you if you didn't give them money; people who had their whole lives packed into a shopping cart; people who were deaf and blind and mentally ill, yelling at the top of their lungs; people doing drugs right out in the open. It was dark and scary.

The handful of underfunded and overextended shelters and soup kitchens located within the heart of Skid Row regularly run out of food and have to turn people away, so we saw people getting so frustrated and angry that they were looking to start fights with anyone who crossed their path. We saw a few other missionaries, feeding and ministering to the homeless, but there was very little police presence. The few cops we did see were either trying to move the homeless along or arrest them. It was a leap of faith just to be there, because you knew you were taking your life into your own hands.

Thankfully, we were always in the presence of Brother Mark, our 6-foot-3 guardian angel in a Houston Astros baseball cap who accompanied us whenever we went into Skid Row. Brother Mark had come up through the Set Free program and was now an assistant pastor. A larger-than-life

African-American guy in his mid-forties, Brother Mark always wore that Astros cap, along with glasses, a Ralph Lauren Polo, baggy jeans, and scuffed-up (but nice) sneakers—he looked like Bay Area rapper E-40, for you hip-hop nerds out there. He loved to talk about God and was constantly thanking Jesus for saving his life. A couple of days into the trip, while we were handing out hot dogs and sodas to the homeless in Skid Row, he turned to me and said, "See that dumpster over there. I lived in and around that dumpster for the better part of twelve years."

I was taken aback. "Wait, you *lived* there? In that dumpster?"

"Yeah," he said. "I did so many nasty, dirty, unbelievably scary things back then. I would marry illegal immigrants for cash to buy drugs. I would commit prostitution in the porta-potties for cash to buy drugs. I would thieve and threaten and hurt people for cash to buy drugs. I would shoot up in the back of a church service. It was the people from Set Free that fed me and talked to me and prayed with me who got me to realize that I wanted to change my life and begin my walk with God."

He told me that, back when he was a homeless drug addict, he was known on the streets of Skid Row as "Monster Mark." He had been sober and off the streets for a couple of years now and, because of Set Free, his whole identity had changed. He had emerged from the heart of darkness to become a pastor who wanted to live his life for God rather than for drugs and sex and theft. I bonded with Brother Mark more than anybody on that trip. It was an honor to have the opportunity to get to know this man who had won this incredible victory over homelessness and addiction. More than anything, I just had so much respect for him because his faith was so authentic.

I had never met anyone like Brother Mark, had never known anybody who relied, trusted, and talked about God and his Christian faith in the way that he did. It was the authenticity of who he was and the transformation he had gone through that was so inspiring. He had every reason to be bitter and cynical about the raw deal life had handed him, yet he felt no anger or resentment for the life he had endured. All he felt was gratitude for the grace and mercy of God. How could you not be inspired? That's where I started to feel like, whatever this is, I want to be a part of it forever. I want to be a part of transforming people's lives.

Until this experience, my Christianity was never truly authentic. Even though I was raised in a Christian home, had gone to a Christian college, and had grown up in a family that was very involved in our church, this type of organization and the work they were doing was very foreign to me. It was unspoken, but the message I had grown up with in my own church was clear: You can give money to help the homeless, but you definitely don't touch homeless people, much less wade into the filth and human misery of a place like Skid Row. In the Bible, and in Christian terms, grace and mercy are the foundation of salvation, but I realized that I hadn't truly understood what that meant until this trip. Being able to see that grace and mercy in a three-dimensional way through the impact that Set Free had on the lives of Brother Mark and so many others was eye-opening.

For Matt and I, the trip had a profound impact on our identities both as Christians *and* as entrepreneurs. We had never experienced anything like it before. Being on the streets, talking to these people, getting to know them, seeing firsthand the darkness and insanity of Skid Row, but also seeing the flip side where this man who lived in a dumpster for twelve years was now a pastor ministering to the people where he once lived, was life-changing. The trip was so transformative that we wanted to make the work we had been doing there a permanent part of our lives.

We knew Nashville had its own rising homeless crisis and, towards the end of the trip, a light bulb went off. Matt and I started to think: What if we used our business as a tool and a resource that actually changed people's lives? How cool would that be? Suddenly it wasn't just about designing funny T-shirts; it was about building a platform to spread love to and raise money and awareness for the most vulnerable and marginalized people in our underserved communities. We wanted to make grace and mercy not just a part of our lives, but a part of our business model.

The thing that sealed the deal for us was that we found out Set Free was already in the process of planting a church in

East Nashville, which was an area we were very familiar with. That was where the dream of building a business that changed people's lives truly began to take shape and become our reality, because we could now partner with a chapter of Set Free in Nashville. We knew that we wanted to do something great and that we wanted to do something that was going to be world-changing, so the fact that they were launching a chapter of Set Free right in my hometown seemed so much more significant than just a mere coincidence. We *knew* this was what we were supposed to do.

By the time I got back to Nashville, our vision had begun to take shape and was becoming not just an idea, but an actionable plan. We would design Nashville-themed T-shirts and use the money from those sales to help the homeless in our own community. All roads had been leading us to this place at this point in time. It was a deeply spiritual moment, where it felt like Matt and I and God were shaking hands. If I hadn't been laid off in Indianapolis, if I hadn't been fired from State Farm, if Matt's trip hadn't been canceled at the last minute, we might never have connected the dots between our core values and our business model. Before this trip, we had a company—now we had a mission to change the world.

CHAPTER 4

Be the Change

"Every single day, in every walk of life, ordinary people do extraordinary things."

—JIM VALVANO

When I got back from Los Angeles, I wrote an open letter to my close friends and family back in Indiana telling them about the incredible and transformative journey I had just undertaken. I could still taste the ashes of Skid Row in my mouth and I wanted to share how deeply I'd been impacted with everyone in my life. I was not the same purposeless young man who had left Indiana in search of his true path. I now had a mission. All my life, I had felt this pull to be a part of something that changed the world, and now I finally knew what it was I was being called to do. I wanted to dedicate my life to helping others and become an agent of positive change in the world.

Our late-night Huggable Tees hangouts, sharing cheap beer and wings and playing video games, turned into late-night brainstorming sessions for how to get a fledgling social enterprise off the ground—without any start-up money. We were aware that there was a growing movement of companies with a socially responsible mission (the most famous at the time was TOMS, which has a one-for-one model), and we began researching all the other companies out there that had some form of do-good business model. What we learned was that profitability and positive social impact are not mutually exclusive. In fact, the more we read and researched, the more we realized that this vision we had of building a successful company and using it as a platform to help the homeless wasn't such a crazy entrepreneurial plan. There was an emerging market of consumers who wanted to know that the companies they chose were doing more than just providing a product or service. More and more, they were looking for companies that do good in the world and whose values aligned with their own.

Matt and I came up with a business plan and immediately began working on setting up a website. But that wasn't enough; we wanted to start helping people struggling with poverty and addiction in our own community right away. A few days after we got back, a bunch of us who had been on the trip to Skid

Row went down to East Nashville to attend Sunday service at Set Free. Both the church and the men's homeless shelter were housed in a raw warehouse space that had once been an egg-sorting factory located in the heart of the largest public housing complex in Nashville. Cayce Homes is the projects. You have families and single parents struggling to make ends meet live alongside people who are drunk and high and acting crazy. Incomes are low, poverty and crime rates are high, and the homeless are cold and hungry. Set Free is the light in the darkness of this part of town. They are there to serve and love on and take care of these people in the community where they live and struggle on a daily basis.

After the service, I introduced myself to the two pastors who ran both the church and the homeless shelter. I explained that we had just come back from a mission trip with Kairos to help their mother church in Los Angeles serve the homeless in Skid Row. I told them about our plan to start a Nashville-based T-shirt company, that we intended to donate the profits to Set Free, and that eventually we also wanted to teach the men coming through the program the skill of screen-printing and hire them to print the shirts.

Pastor Marty and Pastor Kenny were some of original guys who had come through the program back when it was first founded. They were a couple of roughneck bikers from Southern California who had been in and out of prison and homeless

Set Free Church, 816 S. 6th St. Nashville. August 2012. Hundreds of homeless men and women lived here. They received food, clothing, and shelter.

shelters for years before Set Free got them off the streets and helped them rehabilitate their lives. Now in their mid-forties, they were carrying on the Set Free mission with their own homeless rehabilitation ministry. I remember standing in that hot and steamy former-factory-turned-church, trying to explain our business plan and convey the seriousness of our commitment to these two men who had been working in the trenches of homeless outreach for decades. They did not take me seriously.

These guys had been with Set Free since the early '90s. They were used to rich, white do-gooders (with short attention spans) trying to rescue them. Kairos is a ministry for young people that is part of a larger Southern Baptist mega-church in Brentwood, a wealthy suburb outside of Nashville. Matt and I were a couple of blue-collar kids from the Midwest, so we weren't exactly their typical congregants but, to Pastor Marty and Pastor Kenny, we were just a couple of young bucks fresh out of college who showed up at their church one Sunday with a crazy plan to sell T-shirts as a way to change the world.

Within a few weeks, Matt convinced his boss in Owensboro to let him keep working for them from Nashville and, by Labor Day, he had moved in with me. It just so happened that my roommate had decided to move to Alabama to attend seminary and get his master's degree in theology. With the housing market in a slump, he was going to lose a ton of money if he tried to sell the condo, so he offered to rent the place to us. It was a win-win for all of us—but it was especially a blessing for me because my credit was terrible and I had no income, so I doubt anyone else would have rented to me.

Now that we were living together, Matt and I were able to begin serving at Set Free in earnest. We believed in their church and in what they were doing. We weren't married. We didn't have kids. We had time to give and we were inspired, so we got involved hands-on. The pastors were from the streets and didn't really have the organizational skills that Matt and I had, so we came alongside to encourage them and be a resource. We led Bible studies. We hung out with the guys living in the dormitory. We started a Wednesday night church service. When we weren't at the church, we were out there hustling connections for food, clothes, and other essential supplies to help feed not just the homeless, but hundreds of people living in the neighborhood as well. We would hear about a need and we would respond in any way we could to fill it.

In the beginning, of course, most of the people who had been on the trip to Skid Row were on board with our mission of change. We were all on this high coming back from the trip and there was excitement and enthusiasm for our plan. Most of them did show up at that first service at Set Free but then, as the weeks went by and Matt and I were getting more and more involved, we were seeing all the other people from the mission trip slowly start to fade out. Meanwhile, we were just getting started. We knew this was a long-term thing and we were in it for the long haul.

Matt and I were at the church three or four times a week, so we got to know Pastor Marty and Pastor Kenny pretty well. They were twice our age, so they ended up becoming like our cool older uncles. They taught us the Bible and walked with us in our Christian faith. These guys never graduated eighth grade. They were former addicts and con artists. They may not have had the resources to attend seminary or get a degree in theology, yet they were both phenomenal Bible scholars. It was a miracle from God for them to have that intellect of the Bible.

About a month in, we had begun meeting with a web developer we had found on Craigslist to get the site up and running. We were ready to launch, but we still didn't have a name for the company. We'd been chewing on a couple of ideas around the word "project" because it had that give-back feel we wanted to convey and we felt it spoke of a business with a purpose. On the mission trip to Skid Row, we had ministered to a guy named John Wesley, so we were toying with the idea of calling the company The John Wesley Project. For weeks, we had been getting up early and going down to Set Free to do Bible study and then, one morning, the name just popped into my head.

"Matt!" I called out. "I got it...Project 615!"

I think he grumbled back something that sounded like an agreement—it was six o'clock in the morning, a bit early for him to fully appreciate my divine inspiration—but the name took hold of us. 615 is the area code for Nashville, so it firmly rooted us in the community and sent the message that our business was a mission to change the lives of people in Nashville for the better.

We began the design process with one simple question in mind: What will people want to wear that's cool? We decided to make T-shirts that you would find at mall shops like Urban Outfitters because we wanted people to be drawn to our designs regardless of whether our company had a philanthropic mission. The fact that their purchase dollars were also going directly towards tangibly changing people's lives would just be the cherry on top of a very cool graphic.

We ended up launching six or seven Nashville-themed T-shirt designs on the Project 615 website in the fall of 2010, but the very first shirt we designed as Project 615 was a (country music) take on one of my all-time favorite T-shirt graphics. It was a simple list of names in Helvetica that read:

Johnny&
Merle&
Willie&
Waylon&
Hank

We started selling a few shirts here and there and we were slowly building the brand but, in order to truly generate meaningful income for Set Free in the short term, we needed to be able to sell in bulk. So we came up with the idea of printing custom shirts for churches and ministries in and around Nashville. We figured we could generate more revenue when a church ordered 150 shirts printed with their logo than we could trying to sell one at a time. We organized a little pop-up shop at Kairos where we sold our Project 615 designs and told the story of our mission to help the homeless—and then added, "Hey, by the way, we also custom print shirts for people too." We had no capital to invest in our own screen-printing equipment, so we used our connections from Cannonball Creative to get our custom shirts printed. We had been doing work for screen-printing shops all over the country and already had all these relationships going, so we would just trade. Instead of sending out an invoice for $500 worth of design work, we'd call these guys and say, "If you print our Project 615 shirts for us, we'll call it even."

Over the next few months, we did a few more pop-ups, we started taking in more and more orders for custom shirts, and people were buying our original designs online. Next thing you know, we had over a thousand dollars in the bank. As soon as we hit $2,000, I immediately wrote a check and literally ran it over to Set Free. I still vividly remember running down the street with the most pure sense of excitement and joy, like a child who was able to afford his first candy bar. It was bigger than that, even. Clutching that check in my hand, I felt like Charlie when he finds the golden ticket to Willy Wonka's chocolate factory after years of being poor and wishing for something better. When I proudly handed that check to Pastor Kenny, he just looked at me like, "*Really? You want to give this to us?*" It was so validating. I believed in my heart that God had this plan for me, but it wasn't until the moment that I handed that check over to Pastor Kenny that all my lingering doubts and fears disappeared.

I think a big part of what contributed to that sense of excitement was that I had wanted for so long to be a part of something that impacted the world in a meaningful way—going all the way back to that day at the radio station when everyone was going crazy over Kobe breaking the scoring record, and all I could think was that I wanted to do more with my life than talk about sports stats. It wasn't just about the work we had been doing over the last couple of the months; it was about the tangible realization of a lifelong dream.

We were pretty naïve and inexperienced businessmen back then, but even we quickly realized it was going to take a lot more work than what we were generating through the Project 615 website to support both our mission *and* ourselves. Matt was still working his day job for the design firm in Owensboro—which he hated, but it was paying his bills. I was back to collecting unemployment (which had been extended, thanks to the national recession/unemployment crisis). If we wanted out of our present circumstances, we needed a moneymaker that kept the lights on. So we decided to keep building Cannonball Creative as a business alongside Project 615.

That ushered in a deeply creative period where, once again, Matt and I were staying up late, sharing beers, smoking cigars, and hashing over ideas. Our biggest question was the size of our market. I mean, how many people *really* were going to buy Nashville-themed T shirts? (Little did we know.) We got a free-standing whiteboard and put it in our dining room. One side was for Cannonball Creative and the other side was for Project 615. We were brainstorming ideas for both companies—taking breaks in the small hours of the night to play video games and keep chatting, of course. And then, during the day, we were also going downtown to feed and serve and do Bible study with the men at Set Free.

Eventually, we settled on the idea of designing shirts as Cannonball Creative for youth softball and cheerleading teams. We were pragmatic about the growth potential of a philanthropic, Nashville-themed apparel company, so we were envisioning that Cannonball would be our bread and butter and we would use the profits from that business to build both companies. We created this side business where we would travel to softball tournaments and cheerleading events all over the country and set up shop as custom designers of fine youth athletic apparel.

For the next twenty-four months, we were grinding it out on the road for Cannonball, while simultaneously trying to build the Project 615 brand. During the week, we were working for both companies (on top of all the volunteering we were doing at Set Free) and then, every other weekend, twenty-six times a year, we were packing up our cars and driving hundreds of miles to softball tournaments and youth athletic events in Mississippi, Louisiana, Texas, Georgia, Alabama, and Kentucky. Most weekends, though, we were in Mississippi...and there ain't much to do in Mississippi.

Meanwhile, we were a couple of young, single dudes living in Nashville and we weren't enjoying anything the city had to offer because we were on the road nonstop hawking shirts that said "Softball Swag" and "Softball Is My Life" to teenage girls and softball parents. We ended up building a little business that was doing well, but it was in a market that we didn't want to be in and had no passion for. We were trying to build both companies at the same time, selling Cannonball merch to keep the Project 615 dream alive, but we were spending all this time and effort on the road when what we really wanted was to focus on our mission to help the homeless in Nashville.

We had got to the point where we were shipping out orders a couple of times a week for Project 615 and we were custom printing for anyone and everyone who needed shirts (family reunions, bachelorette parties, local bands, non-profits, churches), but we were stalled out on how to take the company to the next level. We were working out of our apartment and bartering design work to get our shirts printed, but if we wanted to really build the business, we would need a dedicated space and our own screen-printing equipment—neither of which we could afford.

From time to time, we would set up as Project 615 at events in and around Nashville. Set Free was supported financially by a Baptist mega-church in Brentwood. A couple of times a year, they would host a ministry fair where local non-profits and philanthropic enterprises could set up tables and booths to generate awareness and involvement among parishioners. Because of all the work we had been doing for Set Free, they would allow us to set up shop at these fairs. We'd sell a few T-shirts and tell the story of our mission to help the ever-growing homeless community in Nashville.

So it was on a cold, gray Sunday morning in early 2012 that a woman came by our table and changed the game for us. She had heard a lot about Set Free as a member of the church, and told us that she was looking to get more plugged in with homeless outreach. She said she wanted to help in any way she could, and asked us to come back to the church the following Tuesday to tell her more about Project 615 and the work we had been doing with Set Free. Matt and I went into that meeting somewhat prepared to articulate our vision of the company and told her about our long-term plan to apprentice the men from Set Free and teach them the trade of screen-printing. When we were done, she said, "I love it," and wrote us a check right then and there for $5,000.

It was never a part of our plan to ask for money or solicit donations for Project 615. We were happy to take the long road and create products that people wanted to buy as a way to bring about social change. We had been slowly trying to build Cannonball and use those profits to expand both businesses but, in two years, we had never even come close to generating that amount of money in one fell swoop. We had been outsourcing all our printing, but that wasn't a sustainable model if we wanted to grow. Five thousand dollars was a game changer. When she handed us that check, it was a total Wayne and Garth moment, where Matt and I wanted to bow down and chant, "We're not worthy," over and over.

We had already researched and priced out what we would need to set up our own screen-printing studio, and used the money to purchase some decent used equipment we had been eying on Craigslist. This was a huge turning point in the evolution of Project 615 because it meant we could finally begin the mission of employing people and giving them a trade. We had been doing our best to support Set Free and their homeless recovery mission, but now we could truly effect sustained, long-term change in these men's lives. That was part of the very genesis of the mission that was conceived on the streets of Skid Row. It was two years in the making—now all we needed was a place to set up shop.

CHAPTER 5

Offer Hope

"Only a life lived for others is a life worthwhile."

—ALBERT EINSTEIN

Next door to the old converted factory where Set Free held their church services and housed the men coming through the homeless recovery program was a two-story brick church that had sat boarded up and abandoned since the 1980s. Some of the homeless men living in the dormitory had pushed in and started sleeping there, so one day, Matt and I snuck in to check out the space. Every room was jammed with dusty furniture and stacks of boxes filled with worn-out Bibles, faded photographs, old hymn books, church directories, Christian books, church bulletins, and secretary files dating back to the early '70s. It was like a time capsule that told the story of a church once filled with hundreds of faithful congregants that had succumbed to the same poverty and blight that took hold of the surrounding neighborhood.

Down a dark and narrow flight of stairs was an eight-hundred-square-foot space that the church had probably used for Sunday school. There was no electricity or heat. We could hear rats scurrying across the cement floor. It was dark and dirty and cold. There was garbage everywhere and it smelled awful. It wasn't exactly a dream space, but Matt and I didn't see a dirty, dingy basement. We saw an opportunity to grow our company and set up a print shop and office.

The church, as well as the Set Free dormitory next door and the house across the street where Pastor Marty lived with his family, belonged to a retired pastor. He had moved away decades ago and rarely ever came around. The church had been abandoned for so long, we figured he might not even notice if we set up our printing equipment in the basement. When we told Pastor Kenny and Pastor Marty what we were thinking, their attitude was basically: Project 615 has been supporting our mission for the past two years; if you guys need this space to grow the business and hire our men, sure, we'll help you sneak in and set up shop. Set Free pastors are not buttoned-up seminary guys. They're not averse to breaking a few rules. Their

The abandoned church next door to Set Free that was Project 615's first head-quarters. It was formerly Woodcock Baptist Church, which had thrived in the 1960s and 1970s before sitting empty and boarded up for decades.

mindset was basically: better to beg for forgiveness later than to ask for permission now.

They let us run extension cords between the two build-ings so we could hang some lights and we began clearing out the basement. As word got around that we had pushed into the church and were trying to set up a screen-printing studio in the basement, we started to get guys from the Set Free dormitory coming by and offering to help us out. One guy would come in, and then another, and, pretty soon, we had a handful of men working for us. We had no money, so we were paying them in cigarettes, McDonald's, and their favorite energy drinks. A lot of these guys were good with their hands, so they were helping us knock down walls, build shelves, clear out furniture and old junk, and set up the press. Up to then, we had been outsourcing everything except our designs, but now we were finally in a position to bring everything, from printing to shipping, in-house. We started teaching the guys the art of screen-printing even as we were learning it ourselves, so there was a lot of trial and error in those early months.

By the end of that year, Matt and I were running on fumes. For two and a half years, we had been burning the candle at both ends, trying to build both businesses and stay true to our day-to-day mission of helping the men at Set Free. So when we were invited to join a mission trip to Haiti, it was more than just an opportunity to expand the Project 615 mission beyond homeless outreach in our backyard, it was a chance to recharge our batteries and find new inspiration.

We had kept in touch with one of the pastors from Set Free California. Pastor Kirk was close to our age, so we were able to connect with him a little more than some of the other pastors. One day, I got a text from him saying that he was traveling to Haiti to bring Christmas to orphaned children and wondered if Matt and I wanted to join him on the trip. We knew immediately that we *had* to go. There was no question. To fund the trip, we came up with the idea of designing a limited-edition T-shirt and donating 100 percent of the profits towards this mission of bringing Christmas to Haitian orphans. "Take Action, Send

Project 615's mission is to hire people recovering from homelessness, addiction, and mental illness. We hired men who were living at Set Free Church and trained them in the art of screen-printing. They would walk next door and work in our production department. This guy's name is Chris Dugger. A Nashville native, Chris found himself battling a drug addiction that led him to being homeless.

Love" was our very first campaign and, looking back, it was very amateur and very broken. It wasn't that well-planned and we didn't market it well, but we probably sold 150 shirts and raised a little under $3,000—enough to fund the trip and fill five suitcases with toys and candy for the children.

On December 26, we boarded a plane bound for Haiti. This was our first time ever being out of the country, so Matt and I were both experiencing the same sense of nervous anticipation. It was both exciting and terrifying stepping off the plane in Port-au-Prince. I remember standing outside the airport with Matt, huddling around all our suitcases filled with Christmas gifts for the children, waiting for Pastor Kirk and our guide to arrive. It was blazing hot and the locals were staring at us. We were two white guys from the Midwest in baseball caps and backpacks; we didn't exactly blend in. After about ten minutes, we started to notice that there were all these big Haitian men hanging around outside the airport staring at us too. We weren't sure if they were the taxi drivers, Haitian mafia, or members of a street gang. After another twenty or thirty minutes with no sign of our guide, Matt and I were beginning to feel genuinely concerned for our safety.

We had no idea what to do. I had emailed ahead with our flight information, but now that we were actually in Haiti, we realized that we had no one we could call. By this point, a couple of the men had begun calling out to us in broken English. As they were slowly pressing in on us, asking for money and where we were going, Matt and I were drawing closer and closer together—to the point where we were practically hugging each other. Then all of a sudden, we hear the *wah-wah* of a horn and a friendly voice calling out, "What's up, guys?" It was Pastor Kirk, leaning out the passenger window of a brightly painted tap tap, one of the (mechanically dubious) trucks and buses that serve as shared taxis in Haiti. All we could think was: *Thank God.*

We piled all our bags into the tap tap and embarked on a three-hour drive along winding dirt roads to the rural village where the orphanage was located. It was hotter than noon on the 4th of July and we were bouncing up and down the whole way. Matt and I kept looking at each other like, "What did we sign up for?" But as we pulled up to the orphanage just after sunset and saw the beautiful faces of the 150 children who had come out of their bunks to greet us, everything else receded into the background and our anxieties vanished. Our driver parked the tap tap and, the moment we stepped off the truck, we were immediately engulfed by the children, who wanted to greet, hug, kiss, high-five, and basically just be with us. I turned to Matt and said "This must have been what the Beatles felt like when they landed in America for the first time."

For the next five days we lived, ate, laughed, played, and prayed with the children at the orphanage. We shared with them the Christian story of the first Christmas and gave them the toys and candy we had brought from home. Every morning, we woke at 5:00 a.m. to the beautiful sound of angelic voices singing praises to God as all the children gathered together for morning prayers.

Haiti is one of the poorest countries in the world. Nearly 60 percent of the population lives below the poverty line. Many of Haiti's 500,000 orphans either lost or were separated from their families in the catastrophic magnitude-7.0 earthquake that had claimed 250,000 lives and displaced over a million people in 2010. Yet somehow, these children had more joy in their hearts than any American I had ever met. Their faces were lit up with love and positivity at all times.

In the middle of the village was a broken-down basketball hoop. Now, Matt and I are from Indiana; if there's a net, we're gonna shoot hoops. We didn't have a basketball, so we grabbed a partially deflated soccer ball and started goofing around, making jump shots and lay-ups. A couple of the kids from the orphanage started to gather around and watch. We were doing tricks and making shots any kid in America with a hoop in the driveway can sink, but these Haitian children were completely amazed. At first, it was just a handful, but then they went and brought more kids from the village, and then more kids. They even went and got teachers from their classrooms and brought them to come watch us. Pretty soon, we had a huge crowd of people from the village cheering us on like they were watching Larry Bird and Michael Jordan play one-on-one.

If you ever want to feel like a celebrity, visit an orphanage in a third world country. Everywhere we went, we were shadowed by dozens of smiling children, surrounding us with hugs and kisses. We felt like rock stars. They just wanted to be around us, hold our hands, jump on our backs, and play soccer with us. They were so sweet and innocent and joyful. You can't help but fall in love. We had found the inspiration we were looking for. It was similar to our experience in Skid Row in that our eyes were suddenly open and we began to have a vision of how we

Haiti, 2012.

could impact lives beyond our own backyard. Here we thought we were bringing these children presents from America, but the true gifts were the smiles on their beautiful faces and the hope shining in their joyful eyes.

We came back from Haiti energized and with a renewed clarity that the work we were doing really could and did make a difference in people's daily lives. Over the course of that next year, we poured ourselves into our mission and slowly started to build a little momentum. At that point, the bulk of the money coming in was still from softball merch through Cannonball and a steady stream of custom screen-printing clients. But we were also popping out shirts here and there for Project 615 and, slowly but steadily, building a reputation locally as a mission-minded company. Any time we printed shirts for a band, church, or non-profit, we'd let them know we were also a company that hired people recovering from homelessness and addiction.

For a while, we were operating from the church under the radar but eventually, Pastor Marty and Pastor Kenny smoothed things over with the landlord. We had been there for maybe a year and, in in that time, the guys from the dormitory had been doing a lot of landscaping and repairs in and around the building. It had started to look less like an abandoned building and more like the church he remembered in its glory days. He was a very old-school and traditional retired pastor in his seventies. Our kind of guerrilla operation was completely foreign to him, but he believed in the mission of the Set Free ministry and was surprisingly cool with us being in the church. Not only did he agree to let Project 615 keep using it as a base of operations (as long as we kept giving back to Set Free), he also turned a blind eye to the men sleeping there and allowed Set Free to expand into the building and use it as a sanctuary for their Sunday services.

By then, we were able to print everything ourselves, which meant more money coming in for Set Free and more money

Co-founders, Derek Evans and Matt Blinco in 2013. This was our second office after we moved a folding table in the print shop to an abandoned classroom in the church to create an office.

for hires. Most of the print work we had coming in at that point was through Cannonball, but it was paying the bills and the guys didn't care whether they were printing softball shirts or 615 shirts. The ultimate goal was to bring everything from printing to shipping in-house, so as we began to outgrow the basement, we very slowly started to take over more rooms in the church and establish a dedicated headquarters for Project 615. First, we cleaned out a room upstairs and turned it into an office so Matt and I could stop working out of our apartment. Then we took over another room for inventory and shipping. Meanwhile, Cannonball had started to bring in enough revenue that we were able to hire someone to manage that business and travel to all the tournaments, which freed Matt and I up to focus full-time on expanding our vision for the Project 615 brand—which was our true passion.

Once we were on-site full-time, more and more guys were coming next door to apprentice as screen printers. One of the things I am most proud of is that, over the years, we have been able to employ over fifty people recovering from homelessness and addiction through our missional hires program. We offer a second chance to others because God has given a second chance to us. True rehabilitation comes through having people to walk alongside with, and from the dignity that comes with having a sense of purpose. That first year, we were able to hire about ten guys from Set Free...with varying degrees of success. We had an eighteen-year-old-kid who had been kicked out of his parents' house, a sixty-five-year-old who had done time for murder, and every other kind of guy in between. Some of them were motivated to work for us because it got them out of the Set Free Bible classes, but just as many truly believed in our mission and were inspired to do work that mattered. We always tried to send the message that they were now a part of something bigger than themselves. A lot of the guys loved that because it gave them a purpose. Yes, we were helping them to get back on their feet, but they were also helping us to build a business that aspired to change the world.

Robert was one of those guys who came to us early on because he heard what we were doing and wanted to be a part

The Project 615 team with the men at Set Free Ranch in Burns, TN, in 2015. The ranch is the first phase of recovery, where men and women go to get clean and sober from drugs and alcohol.

of something meaningful. He didn't look like your average homeless guy. He was a college-educated, clean-cut, very sweet Southern gentleman who was about my father's age. He had been married for thirty years and had three successful adult children, but he had been struggling with alcoholism for most of his life. Eventually, his wife got fed up with his drinking and left him. After the divorce, his drinking spiraled out of control and he got fired from his management job in the carpentry business. After he lost his wife and his job, his life fell apart and he ended up homeless and living on the street. He tried getting sober and was in and out of rehabilitation facilities, but inevitably he would end up back out on the street, which ultimately led him to Set Free and Project 615.

Robert was one of our first official missional hires. Before we had any money to pay these guys, he was there every single day just as a volunteer who wanted to help out in any way he could. He worked for us for about a year and a half and was instrumental in helping us grow early on. He had been a carpenter for many years and loved working with his hands, so he immediately picked up on the screen-printing and became a true artist. In many ways, he was the poster child for our missional hires. He was a dedicated craftsman, came in on his own time, stayed late, and always aspired to produce the highest-quality work. But, at the same time, he had his own battle going on in the background because he was still struggling with his alcoholism. A couple of months in, he slipped. He started to sneak a couple of drinks and then he just fell into a cycle where he was drinking pretty heavily, coming in late, and doing sloppy work. But he picked himself back up, got clean again, and went back to being a dedicated worker. He even earned back our trust to the point where he ended up running our shipping department.

Then, one Saturday morning, he came in to help us catch up on some orders and he just reeked of alcohol. His speech was slurred and he was stumbling around, knocking things over. Trust and accountability are the pillars of any recovery

(Top) Robert, a Nashville native and one of our very first missional hires.
(Bottom) Project 615 has employed over fifty people recovering from homeless-
ness, addiction, and mental illness since 2010.

program. No matter how much we loved the guy, we couldn't have him drinking on the job. It wasn't easy, but we had no choice but to tell him he couldn't work for us anymore if he wasn't sober. He ended up leaving Set Free and trying to make it on his own. Sadly, this time he wasn't able pick to himself up again. It wasn't long after, maybe a few months later, that a guy who had come through the program reached out to us on Facebook to let us know that Robert had passed away. He just drank himself to death.

One of the things we struggled with early on was this romantic idea we had going in that these men would work for us for a year or two, and then they'd all go out into the world and get jobs, have money in the bank, buy a house, wear a tie to work, and get back with their wives and children. The reality is much more complicated. These men are struggling with some dark demons and there's rarely that kind of fairy-tale ending. We could see all this tangible good that we were doing in their daily lives. We saw guys get sober and pull themselves up from darkness and despair. We were so hopeful that they were going to change their lives for good and, when you end up losing them to their demons, it's heartbreaking.

There was one guy who worked for us for us for an afternoon and then, the next day, he stabbed a woman in the street and went back to jail for the rest of his life. We had guys struggling with addiction who would work for us until they got their first paycheck, and then immediately use it to go buy drugs. There was one guy who had been kicking around the Set Free dormitory for a couple of months. When we heard he was a painter, we offered him fifty bucks to paint our logo on the side of the church. He did an awesome job but, as soon as we gave him the cash, he disappeared and we never heard from him again.

But, for every heartbreak, there were also guys who reminded us of the true purpose of our mission. One of our best screen printers was a veteran who had done three tours in Iraq and came back home with PTSD. Karl had served and sacrificed for his country but, like so many of our veterans, he came home deeply traumatized, didn't get the services he needed to take care of his mental health, and fell through the cracks. He found himself homeless and living on the streets for a little while before getting plugged into Set Free. He worked his way up through the program and, when he came to work for us, we trained him as screen printer. As a military guy, being a part of something bigger than himself and doing work that mattered gave Karl the anchor he needed. He was so disciplined and dedicated that he became one of our managers. He worked for us for almost two years and then his father passed away and he had to move back to his hometown to take care of the rest of the family. We were sorry to lose him because he was a phenomenal screen printer, but we were honored to be that bridge he needed to get back up on his feet. That's the truest kind of success story you can have.

Ultimately, we learned to let go of our expectations and find success in all the small moments along the journey. The change we were offering our missional hires was hope and a solid footing on which to move forward in life. In Robert's case, he ended up stumbling again (and, sadly, it cost him his life), but for that period of time he was working for us, he was the man he was meant to be. Instead of reaching for some elusive finish line, we paid for doctor visits, gave them money to go visit their kids that they hadn't seen in years, paid for meals, and helped them find clothes that fit. We had one guy working for us who wore a size 7X shirt. You can't just go to a store and buy that size, so Matt ordered some shirts online for him from a big-and-tall retailer out of his own pocket (to this day, he still gets their catalog in the mail every month). We would do a lot of these things with our personal money because we just wanted to make their day in some small way. After all, serving the least of these was our calling.

The truth is there's never a definitive crossing-the-finish-line moment. You start a business like ours to change lives, and you think you're going to cross that finish line many, many times but, eventually, you realize that you need to adjust your definition of success. For every guy who pulls his life together and goes on to hold down a steady job or become a pastor, there are countless others who stumble along their journey. It wasn't as romantic as we thought it would be, but what we learned is that having friendships with these men, holding their hands in life, praying with them, crying with them, celebrating with them, and caring for them is the real measure of our accomplishment. The true win is in the process.

CHAPTER 6

Spread Love, It's the Nashville Way

"Not all of us can do great things. But we can do small things with great love."

—MOTHER TERESA

When we conceived the idea of starting a philanthropic company that sold Nashville-themed apparel, never in a million years did we imagine that it would take off the way it did. We knew we were making high-quality, handmade products and that our mission would resonate with our customers, but a big part of what catapulted us from a ragtag screen-print shop in the basement of an abandoned church to a successful business enterprise with dozens of employees and multiple retail stores was that the city itself was in the midst of a major economic boom and cultural renaissance.

We were part of a wave of young and ambitious entrepreneurs who were drawn to Nashville's diversity, rich history, and small-town vibe. Neighborhoods like Germantown and The Gulch—historic districts that had fallen into decline by the end of the 20th century—had experienced an explosion of mixed-use residential and retail developments. Music, arts, and cultural festivals were springing up all over town, bringing Nashvillians together in newly revitalized parks and public spaces. By 2014, there was all this momentum in the city and you started seeing a hundred people moving here a day, which meant more businesses, more construction, and more jobs. In the two years since Project 615 had occupied the church basement, East Nashville had slowly but steadily begun to establish itself as an up-and-coming hub for artists, musicians, and writers, as well as small business owners, restaurants, and tech start-ups. We found ourselves right in the middle of this exciting transformation—a golden era, if you will—and the timing could not have been better.

At the beginning of that year, the guy we had hired to manage Cannonball and travel to all the tournaments left us to take a job selling cars. Initially, that was a huge blow. The last thing Matt and I wanted to do was go back to spending every weekend on the road hustling softball merch. Up to then, Cannonball had been our main source of revenue, which was a blessing because we would never have survived those early years, much less been able to hire and train the guys from Set Free, if we hadn't had all that print work coming in through softball sales. But we had no passion for it. It was one thing to have someone running that business for us but, when it fell back to us to manage on a daily basis, we realized we just didn't want it. At the end of the day, we were only printing and selling those shirts to support the dream of Project 615.

Meanwhile, there was this undeniable energy in the city. Industry was booming. Construction was booming. Retail was booming. The population was exploding. We were no strangers to getting out there and selling shirts, and we started thinking: Why not focus our energy on doing pop-ups for Project 615 at festivals and events in our own city? We'd feel more fulfilled by the work—*and* we'd get to sleep in our own beds at the end of the night. So we made the decision to pull the plug on Cannonball and finally focus all our attention on building Project 615. It felt like a huge risk at the time, but we had come this far trusting our instincts.

At the time, there was no other company like ours in Nashville, or even Tennessee, and the market demand for a mission-minded apparel brand that reflected the attitude and energy of the city kept growing. We began to expand our designs from primarily country music and Tennessee-based themes into positive messaging graphics that reflected our core values and raised money for specific causes. Up to then, we had been giving every single dime we made through Project 615 to Set Free (going into that fourth year, we had donated over $30,000 to the ministry). We would continue to give back to the church and to hire the men to do our printing, but the trip to Haiti had broadened our vision for Project 615 beyond local homeless outreach and we began to shift our model into doing dedicated campaigns for specific causes.

We started partnering with nonprofits like Project HOPE (whose mission is to end human sex trafficking in Southern California) and Show Hope (which helps orphans around the world connect with loving families) to raise money and awareness for their organizations. But we also stayed rooted in the community and maintained our local focus with a targeted campaign where we raised money to help a Nashville family cover the medical and adoption costs of a five-year-old with special needs from China.

Of course, social media played a huge role in getting the Project 615 brand and our message out in to the world. Instagram was a game-changer for us because it allowed us to visually connect our products to our mission in a way that we could never have done otherwise. In addition to showcasing our designs and promoting our campaigns and pop-up events, we posted photos of our missional hires and celebrated their stories of struggle and redemption. Over the course of that year, we steadily built a following on social media and the show of love and support we received in response to our posts infused us with the energy we needed to keep moving forward.

As we started gaining recognition in Nashville for the work we were doing both in the community and for nonprofit organizations, local news channels began reaching out to do features on our company and our mission. Meanwhile, several of the shops and boutiques that were starting to spring up in East Nashville began carrying some of our designs—which was huge for us because it meant we now had a physical presence in stores. For the first time, we started to realize that there was potentially a much bigger market for the 615 brand than just a handful of online T-shirt sales and custom-printing orders. We had been setting up at local festivals and doing pop-ups around the city, with modest sales, but the real turning point came that fall at the city's 25th Annual Oktoberfest, which took place over three days in the heart of (where else?) Germantown. On that particular weekend, Matt had plans to go camping, so I decided to just go and set up on my own. I figured I'd sell a couple dozen shirts, tops, and tell our story; at best, we'd break even and maybe even pick up some new custom clients. I was totally unprepared for the response we got.

Within the first hour, I was totally slammed and had to call a few friends to come down and help me out. Over the course of that weekend, we sold hundreds and hundreds of shirts, but the best part was seeing people's faces lit up by how much they loved our designs and their enthusiastic response to our mission. We had never come close to making that many sales at a single softball tournament, nor had we experienced that kind of energy and love from our customers. Whatever concerns we may have still had about our decision to shut down the Cannonball brand, one thing was for sure: We had followed our passion and the people of Nashville were embracing us.

We were savvy enough to realize that we could use social media as a platform to raise awareness and money for our missions, but we were also humble enough to know that we needed fresh ideas and energy if we wanted to keep growing. We wanted to position ourselves as a brand that sat at the intersection where "fashion meets compassion," so, that spring and summer, we hired two young women just out of college, Lianna and Tayler, who had experience in social media marketing and fashion. These ladies brought a fresh perspective to our missions and marketing campaigns, as well as a passion to do work that matters and keep "fanning the flame." Almost overnight, we went from a bunch of unshaven dudes printing T-shirts in a dimly lit basement to a team of dedicated individuals working together to build a company that we all passionately believed in.

By the end of that summer, we had a couple of successful T-shirt campaigns in partnership with local nonprofits under our belt, but we wanted to close out the year with something bigger that had a global reach. It had been almost two years since our trip to Haiti, so we decided what we really wanted to do was plan and fund our own trip to bring Christmas to orphans in a third world country. The only question was where. We had a brainstorming meeting where we each wrote down the name of the county we most wanted to serve. Every single one of us wrote down the same country: Ethiopia. It was crazy. It must have been meant to be.

The core idea behind the campaign was to bring Nashville to Africa, so we created a design that incorporated our state flag, the Tennessee Tri-Star, and the outline of the African continent. One hundred percent of the proceeds would go towards our mission of bringing Christmas joy to orphans in Ethiopia. We reached out to a local nonprofit in Nashville called Sweet Sleep that was already on the ground in Ethiopia, and they agreed to partner with us so we would have access to their connections and resources. We crunched the numbers and found that, in order to successfully execute a trip of this magnitude, we would need to sell enough shirts to raise $12,000—far more than we had ever generated through any single T-shirt campaign. Basically, we would have to sell at least five hundred shirts in less than a month or our dream of taking the Project 615 mission to Ethiopia would fail before we even got started.

The first official Project 615 T-shirt campaign to provide Christmas to orphans in Ethiopia. Winter 2014.

Lianna came up with the idea of putting together a food truck meet-up to help promote the campaign and boost sales of the shirt we had designed. We reached out to four or five of our favorite food trucks and a dozen local vendors who were also working to have a positive impact on the community. We hired a few local bands that supported our mission to play live music at the event and put the word out on our social media sites. On November 9, 2014, Project 615 hosted its very first Nashvember event in Centennial Park. We were expecting maybe a couple of hundred people to show up but, in the end, over three thousand Nashvillians came out to show their love and support. In one day, we raised $13,000 for our mission trip to Ethiopia.

That was an eye-opening moment for us because it was the first time we realized that not only were people following us on social media, they truly believed in our mission and wanted to be a part of our world-changing movement. The love that we had been pouring into Nashville was coming back to us tenfold. Our mission was always to use our gifts and talents to change the world. Up to then, it had been primarily through local homeless outreach and partnerships with nonprofits, but now we were able to truly expand our reach and begin spreading that good ol'-fashioned Nashville love beyond the physical borders of the city.

The following month, Matt and I went home to Indiana to spend the holidays with our families. On December 26th, we met at the airport in Chicago, where we embarked on the thirteen-and-a-half-hour flight to Ethiopia. I remember just being in awe that we had created this mission trip and had raised the money to fund it solely through sales of our T-shirt designs. We took a selfie to commemorate the moment and posted it on our Instagram page with the caption: "We launched the

Derek and Matt, selfie taken at Chicago O'Hare International Airport.

T-shirt company in 2010 to help change the world never thought we would actually travel the world to help others. Africa here we come."

Unlike the trip to Haiti, where we stayed onsite, for this trip our team of six (myself, Matt, Lianna, Tayler, and two people from Sweet Sleep) stayed in a hotel in the capital so we were able to spend our first couple of days in Ethiopia exploring the city. For a mere ten dollars, we were able to hire a taxi for the entire day and our driver took us on a tour of Addis Ababa, a densely populated, bustling city that is a mix of old and new. Pockets of the city had been modernized, with new construction underway, but many neighborhoods were worn down and access to reliable electricity and potable water was still difficult to come by.

We went to a couple of local restaurants (and invited our driver to join us for dinner) where we sampled traditional Ethiopian food, which is always served with *injera* (a spongy pancake-like sourdough bread that you use instead of silverware to scoop up your food). I'm not the most adventurous eater, especially when I travel (and oddly enough, I couldn't find a Chick-fil-A drive-through anywhere in the capital), so I was relieved to find that the coffee for which Ethiopia is famous is always served with freshly popped popcorn—can you say popcorn and coffee overload?

For the next leg of the trip, Sweet Sleep had arranged for us to visit one of several Ethiopian orphanages that their organization supports. We hired another driver for the day and made the three-hour drive outside the city. Compared to the smog- and exhaust-filled, bustling, chaotic capital, Ethiopia's countryside is a landscape of lush, green, rolling hills and farmland. We arrived at the orphanage, which doubled as a school, armed with suitcases full of toys and candy, and spent a couple of days hanging out with the children, playing soccer and schoolyard games.

Ethiopia has one of the largest orphan populations in the world. Roughly 4.5 million children (about 5 percent of a population of approximately 100 million) have lost one or both of their parents to crippling poverty, famine, or the HIV/AIDS epidemic. The number of AIDS orphans is estimated at around a million children. We were warned that many of the children at the orphanage were infected with the virus themselves, so when playing with them we had to be careful not to expose ourselves. Yet, despite all they had endured, the children had so much joy and love in their hearts. We held their hands, listened to their stories, prayed, laughed, and sang with them. They loved to listen to us talk because they thought our accents were hilarious.

At the end of our last day, as our taxi was pulling away from the village, I looked back at the smiling faces of the children running along behind us and wondered what it would cost to build a school that provided a home and an education for a couple of hundred orphaned children—it was just a handful of basic trailer-like structures. I asked our driver and he said that most of the orphanages in Ethiopia had been built for about $25,000. We had raised half that amount in just one day to fund this trip. It didn't seem so far-fetched to imagine that our next global campaign could be to fund the construction of an orphanage and school like this one.

As much as we loved visiting with the children, one of the highlights of that trip for me was that Sweet Sleep had arranged for us to spend time in a village where we were introduced to single mothers who had started small businesses to provide for their families. In addition to the orphan care that they do around the world, Sweet Sleep also works with women in rural villages and empowers them to start businesses. The idea is that, by supporting these women and providing them with the necessary resources to create a sustainable income, they will be able to afford to feed their families and fewer children will end up as orphans. It was incredible to see this work in action.

These women lived in ramshackle huts made of wood, mud, and sheets of corrugated iron. For the most part, they had no electricity or running water, yet they used all the resources at their disposal (not least of which was their entrepreneurial spirit) to create products that they sold at their local market. We met a woman in her seventies who was supporting multiple generations in her family with her beautiful hand-woven brooms. She didn't speak a word of English, but she beckoned us into her hut where she served us coffee and popcorn. Another woman invited us into her hut, which was filled with brightly colored fabrics that she lovingly sewed into beautiful scarves that she then sold at the market. One of the most surprising ventures we encountered was a woman who made french fries. Sweet Sleep had helped her acquire a deep fryer, and she grew her own potatoes and blended her own spices. It was so surreal to be sitting in a hut in this rural Ethiopian village, eating the most legit-tasting fries that rivaled any you'd find at an American steakhouse.

I felt such a deep affinity with these remarkable women. They had little business training beyond the support they got from Sweet Sleep, nor did they have much formal education of any kind, yet they were true entrepreneurs in every sense of the word. You could see the pride and joy on their faces as they invited us into their homes to view and sample their work. Part of my own journey as an entrepreneur had been learning to embrace the gifts and talents that came naturally to me in order to fully realize the vision I had for Project 615, but these women had figured that out long ago. Their lives were not easy—they had none of the luxuries or creature comforts that we take for granted in the US—yet they instinctively used the talents and resources that were readily available to them to create simple and beautiful products they could sell to support their families.

Our mission to spread love from Nashville to Africa had ended in the most inspirational way possible. We had traveled to Ethiopia hoping to change lives, and yet somehow I felt changed by the indomitable spirit of the incredible women and children we had met there. The biggest lesson I took away from the experience was that, whether you're two guys from the Midwest making T-shirts to change the world or a single mother in Ethiopia making french fries to support your family, doing work that matters is about trusting that desire and passion that drives you to be a part of something bigger than yourself. If you focus on the things that you have a passion for and you truly want to impact the world, it's that energy that is going make what you do even bigger and better.

We were two college buddies who shared a dream of starting a company that changed people's lives, and now we had traveled to Africa because of that dream. This was the first time that we were truly able to use the platform of Project 615 to touch other people's lives on a global level. It was such a powerfully emotional experience for us because we were now in year four of doing this work that we felt called to do, and we were finally seeing the fruits of our labor in a tangible way. Not only that, we were starting to see that our vision was catching on and the city that we called home believed in us as much as we believed in them.

CHAPTER 7

Love Big

"If you want to lift yourself up, lift up someone else."

—BOOKER T. WASHINGTON

The first time I heard the song "Juicy" by the Notorious B.I.G., it completely blew my mind. It was more than just a rags-to-riches song about a young man's rise from poverty into the limelight of fame and fortune; it was an anthem celebrating the universal drive to reach for the stars—no matter how unlikely that dream might seem. At eleven years old, a lot of the lyrics in the song about hustling on the streets of Bed-Stuy, Brooklyn, and living the champagne life as a rap star went completely over my head, but when I heard Biggie rap, "Spread love, it's the Brooklyn way," I instinctively understood what he meant.

Those words resonated with me on a spiritual level and, in many ways, would become a call to action for how I wanted to live my life. They spoke of being rooted in your community and of being a champion for those who live "the struggle" every single day.

As a kid coming of age in the '90s, rap and hip-hop were a powerful influence and source of inspiration in my life. It was the Golden Age of hip-hop and, for kids like me growing up in rough urban communities, it felt so much more vital and relevant than the steady stream of Led Zeppelin and Bob Seger coming out of my parents' stereo. All my life, I had wanted to find a way to incorporate this passion I had into my work and my life, but I could never have foreseen that this passion I had for hip-hop music would become so entwined with my life's mission.

In 2009, when Matt and I first created Cannonball and were trying to create our own original designs, I had the idea to use that lyric from "Juicy," but to substitute Nashville for Brooklyn. Then, in 2012, we officially launched it as a T-shirt for Project 615. Whether it was the design or our utter lack of experience when it came to marketing at that point, the shirt never really caught on and we ended up retiring it a year later. But, even though it was kind of a dud, the phrase and the message behind it stuck with me.

Two years later, we decided to bring it back and reimagine the design for our "Heart for the Hungry" campaign—never thinking that it would catch on the way it did and become an iconic phrase in Nashville. We had just come back from Ethiopia and were so energized by the outpouring of support we had gotten for that campaign that we immediately began planning our missions for the year ahead. Having just successfully executed our first global campaign, our eyes were opened to all the possibilities of what our company could be and grow into. We had already begun moving into a model of dedicated campaigns and had started to build a reputation within the nonprofit community as a retail company that did good work. We decided that we would start partnering with the organizations that had begun reaching out to us and do these types of campaigns quarterly to really make an impact with our business both on a local and a global level.

For our first campaign of 2015, we wanted to harness the love and energy that took us to Africa and bring it back home by working with a Nashville-based nonprofit to help the more than four thousand children living in poverty and suffering from hunger in Middle Tennessee. One of the organizations that had reached out to us looking to partner on a campaign was the Bridge Ministry. In addition to their homeless outreach under the Jefferson Street Bridge on Tuesday nights, they also partner with schools and after-care programs to provide food-insecure and homeless children with food bags on Friday afternoons so that they have meals to eat over the weekend. I couldn't think of a better way to embark on the next phase of our outreach than to partner with the organization that had first introduced me to mission work.

Our model for that campaign was: For every shirt purchased, Project 615 would donate the equivalent of four meals to children suffering from hunger. We had to come up with new shirts for the campaign and "Spread Love, It's the Nashville Way" seemed like the perfect way to inspire awareness of child hunger and homelessness and motivate people to be passionate for the poor. We scrapped the original design and chose a new font that was a little cooler and more rugged, and made it more of an announcement on your shirt of who you are. The plan was to launch the campaign at the end of January—with Valentine's Day right around the corner, this concept of "spreading love" would tie in beautifully to the spirit of the holiday.

That winter was one of the coldest in Middle Tennessee in thirty years. We knew all too well what this meant for the thousands of homeless people living on the streets in Nashville. Now that we had an active community of followers on social media, we wanted to be an advocate for people in times of need, so every so often, we would post about different resources in the community to help raise awareness and spread the word. We'd post about amber alerts in Tennessee to let people in that area know to be on the lookout. In the lead-up to the holidays, we'd provide locations where they could drop off toy donations. In the winter, when the homeless are particularly vulnerable, we'd post links to local organizations that people could call to get help. The day after Valentine's Day, we posted, "It's cold #Nashville, so if you see any folks on the streets, here is how they can get emergency shelter & help. Please RT!" on all our social media platforms and provided a link to the Nashville Rescue Mission.

Some time after 2:00 the following morning, I got a text from one of my best friends from high school:

"Did you see Miley Cyrus posted about you guys?"

Apparently, he had just watched her perform as a musical guest on the *Saturday Night Live 40th Anniversary Special* and then had gone on Instagram afterward and saw that she had taken a screenshot of our post and reposted it on her account. After that, my phone just blew up with texts, calls, emails, and social media tags and alerts from friends and followers letting us know they had seen her regram of our post. What blew my mind about it was that the *SNL* special was a huge, star-studded event. She would have been at an after-party in New York City with celebrity icons like Robert De Niro, Jim Carrey, Paul Simon, Keith Richards, and Paul McCartney, who had all appeared on the show with her. We had no idea that she was even aware of Project 615 but, in the middle of that glitz and glamour, she had taken up our plea to help the homeless in Nashville and helped spread it to the world. The next day, we sent her a shirt to say thank you for the support.

At that moment in time, Miley had captivated people's attention and was very much in the international spotlight, but she was also a homegrown Tennessee artist who was very much rooted in the community where our business was based. It sent a message to the people of Nashville (and the world): If someone like Miley Cyrus cares about homeless people, then *we* should care too. Her regram of our post drove a lot of traffic to our website and social media platforms but, more meaningfully to us than that, it inspired a round of applause from our customers who were shouting us out on their social media. It was just a simple thing that she did, but it was such a cool affirmation for a company like ours. A simple repost tells us, "Hey, you guys are awesome. Keep up the great work." You need that as a start-up business, especially one like ours that is very hands-on with people who are suffering from homelessness, addiction, and mental illness, because it ain't easy.

When an international celebrity regrams something positive that you are trying to put out into the world, and draws that level of attention to it, you enjoy the moment. Then you take a deep breath, wake up the next morning, and keep rolling. By March, we had raised over a thousand meals for hungry children through our "Heart for the Hungry" campaign with the Bridge Ministry. As winter turned to spring, we launched our next campaign, "Freedom Is," in partnership with ONEless Ministries to raise funds and awareness for the fight to end human trafficking. It felt like we were growing and gaining all this momentum as a brand, but I was about to be reminded that running an apparel company out of the basement of an abandoned church was not exactly an ideal situation.

Sometime in mid-April, I was in my office making some calls when there was a knock on the door. Lianna, who had been in the inventory room preparing to ship out some orders, poked her head in and whispered, "I think you need to come and take a look at the inventory room. There's some...bugs in there." We were in an abandoned church—of course there were bugs—there were insects and other vermin all over the building.

I put my hand over the receiver. "I'm on the phone," I said, and waved her off. A few minutes later, she knocked on the door again.

"Derek," she said, more insistent this time. "I really think you need to come and look *now*."

There was an urgency in her tone that made me hang up the phone immediately. It finally registered that whatever was going on was bigger than the usual pests we dealt with on a daily basis. I followed Lianna into our inventory/shipping room and it only took half a second to register that there were literally thousands upon thousands of termites crawling over every inch of the room. They were on the windows, the shelves, the walls, the floor. It took another half second to register that they were also all over the boxes that were filled with over a thousand shirts that we had just printed and carefully packed and folded.

"Quick!" I called out to anyone within earshot. "Start moving the boxes!"

Our headquarters were not pretty by any stretch of the imagination—there were feral cats and mice scurrying around all over the place, homeless guys smoking in every part of the building, cords running everywhere—but the inventory room was where our gold was. We had to protect that room because, if anything happened to our shirts, there would be no money coming in. Matt appeared in the doorway and there was a look of horror on his face as he took in the plague of termites that had descended on our precious inventory.

"Run over to Set Free," I shouted, "and get anybody you can to help us start moving the boxes into a different room!"

By that point, I was freaking out as Lianna and I rushed to grab whatever we could and move it out of harm's way. The building had been both a blessing and curse. The fact that the landlord had allowed us to piggyback on Set Free's lease meant that we could keep giving back to the ministry even as we were trying to grow as a brand, but trying to run a legitimate business out of a rundown and now termite-infested building was a nightmare. It was freezing in the winter, stifling hot in the summer, and something was always leaking or breaking down. The frustration that had been simmering under the surface for years about our less-than-ideal workspace started to boil over and turn to anger. We had invested so much time, hard work, and money into this inventory—even if we managed to get all the shirts out before the termites did any damage, how long before another catastrophe struck?

I remember, at one point, just standing there in the middle of all the chaos, thinking: Where in the world are we going to put all this inventory? We only had a limited amount of space in the church and we had pretty much expanded into every room that we could. That's when I felt a buzz on my cell phone. Thankful for any kind of distraction, I pulled it out of my back pocket and checked my email. There was a message congratulating us on being approved for a retail space in The Shoppes on Fatherland, a retail development of twenty-plus locally owned stores that had sprouted up near Five Points, an up-and-coming hipster neighborhood in East Nashville about a half-mile from our headquarters at Set Free.

Back when it first opened in 2013, they had reached out to us and asked if we were interested in opening a store. Matt thought it would be cool to have our own little retail space. I think my response was something like, "Yeah, sure—when pigs fly." The idea of Project 615 opening a store at that point was basically like imagining moving into a mansion in Beverly Hills. In 2013, we were barely selling a couple of shirts a week online, let alone enough to justify opening a brick-and-mortar location.

I have to credit Matt for not giving up on the idea. A year later, he convinced me to at least look into it, but by the time we had inquired, every store was full. We put our name on the waiting list and then basically forgot all about it. We never even said the word "retail" again.

There's so much in business that is unknowable. There are so many factors that can set a start-up back or push it forward to the next level—and we'd had our share of both—but there is one thing I *do* know with absolute certainty: If the termites hadn't invaded our inventory room, we never would have been motivated to open our first store. It was an incredibly spiritual moment. If that email had come a month, a week, maybe even just a day earlier, without a doubt, we would have turned it down. The rent was $495 a month (plus $45 for utilities), which, at that point, seemed like it might as well have been $495 million. It seemed inconceivable back then that we could afford to take on a financial commitment like that—especially when we could use that money to invest in our inventory or donate it back to a nonprofit. But the moment that message came up on my phone, it was like a blessing from God because I realized that we could move all of our inventory to the store—and then no termites would be on our shirts. In the space of less than ten minutes, I had experienced horror and panic, bitterness and anger, and now joy and excitement.

Unfortunately, we couldn't move right into the space. The previous occupant had sixty days to finish out their lease and move out before they gave us the keys, and then we had to build it out. So we moved the inventory to a temporary location in the church. Then we moved it back after a few of the guys from Set Free helped us remove the rotting wood and an exterminator had bombed the room to get rid of the termites. The lead-up to opening the store was such a whirlwind of planning and activity that I can barely remember much, other than this overwhelming sense that we had just taken the business to an entirely new level. We had moved into uncharted territory, and those weeks were marked by a mixture of giddy excitement and absolute terror.

To promote the store, we decided to throw an opening-day launch party. We put the word out on our social media that we were having a grand opening and announced that the first one hundred people in line would get a free poster and discounts on future purchases. We hired a DJ and food vendors, and set up a tent, tables, and balloons outside so the event would have a fun and festive block-party vibe. At 11:00 am on June 20, we officially opened for business. I don't know what we were expecting, but the turnout exceeded our wildest dreams. Throughout the day, it was a steady stream of people showing up to support the opening. Even my parents made the four-and-a-half-hour drive from Indianapolis to surprise me.

The grand opening of our first store, located at 1006 Fatherland St. The turn-out exceeded our wildest dreams.

(Top) Grand opening traffic. (Bottom) Some of our first customers.

In addition to all the people in the community, friends, neighbors, and family members who came out for the event, hundreds of the people who followed us on social media turned out to show their support. It was beautiful thing to feel this outpouring of love from our fans and customers. Suddenly, they weren't just names in a comment on Instagram or Facebook; they were real people that were shaking our hands, slapping us on the back, and telling us they loved our company and our shirts. It was incredible to see their faces, talk to them, and have the opportunity to thank them in person for their support over the years. It was a moment of clarity and affirmation, like God was slapping us on the butt and saying, "Attaboy! Now keep going!"

At the end of the day, we counted up the receipts and found we had made enough money to cover rent on the store for the next two years. We were blown away. We had done pop-ups at dozens of different events over the years, and that was the most money we had ever made in a single day purely through T-shirt sales. It was another one of these moments where we realized we had completely underestimated our potential. The shop was 192 square feet and, when we signed the lease, we honestly weren't sure we could generate enough sales to support a space that size. But by the end of that day, we knew we had already outgrown it. When a four-hundred-square-foot space opened up in the same retail complex towards the end of that year, we jumped on it. It was only about ten feet away, but we went from being located in a side alley to being right on Fatherland Street, so we were now visible to all the shopping traffic coming through the neighborhood.

Year five is make-or-break time for a small business. We knew all too well the survival stats out there for start-ups: 20 percent of all small businesses fail in their first year; 30 percent fail in the second year; and 50 percent fail after five years. To be in a position where we were not just surviving, but thriving and growing, was incredible—and we owed it all to the people of Nashville who embraced us and to the support of our fans, followers, and customers.

Later that year, Miley posted a selfie on her Instagram page wearing the "Spread Love, It's the Nashville Way" shirt we had sent her back in February as a thank-you for regramming our post about helping the homeless in Nashville get through the winter. That was the first time a celebrity posted a photo on social media wearing one of our shirts, and it created even more buzz and excitement around the Project 615 brand and the core message of our company. Miley may have been the first but, in the years to come, we would have sightings of everyone from Carrie Underwood to Garth Brooks in our designs.

To this day, however, nothing can quite compare to the excitement I felt the day Lady Gaga was spotted wearing the "Spread Love" tee—in Nashville, no less. Matt and I were actually out of town because we had taken a couple of team members to a leadership conference in Atlanta. We had pulled up to the hotel at about 4:00 in the afternoon. As we were checking in, I started getting notifications that people were tagging Project 615 in photos they were posting on Instagram. I checked my personal account and I had a couple of direct messages from friends saying, "Dude, Lady Gaga's walking around town wearing your shirt!"

My phone was blowing up and Matt and I were looking at each other like, "No freakin' way. There's no way this is true." But, sure enough, it was. When I got up to my room, I went online and there was video footage all over the Internet of Lady Gaga stepping out of an old-school Ford Bronco wearing a pink cowboy hat and our "Spread Love" tee. It turned out that one of the co-writers for her new song "Million Reasons" was from Nashville, so she had decided to kick off her Dive Bar Tour—a series of pop-up concerts in small venues across the country to promote her upcoming album. Now here she was outside The 5 Spot in East Nashville, literally down the street from the new store on Fatherland, wearing our shirt. It was like a massive billboard broadcasting our core mission and message to the world.

As the day went on, there was more news coverage of Gaga driving around town, posing for photos with her fans. Then, throughout the night, people were posting and tagging us in more photos and videos. Gaga herself was even Snapchatting from her hotel room with the shirt on. And, through the miracle of social media, we were able to watch the whole thing happening in real time from our hotel in Atlanta. It was absolutely insane.

Every once in a while, we'll mail some of our designs to celebrities—hoping our message will resonate with them and they'll wear it—but we had no idea Lady Gaga even had that shirt. We were all so tickled, but I think I was more giddy than everyone else because I had dreamed that shirt into existence and it had so much personal significance for me. It was this idea that was deep down inside of me, going all the way back to when I was an eleven-year-old kid in Indiana listening to "Juicy" for the first time. It was the model by which I tried to live my life and the foundation upon which we had built the company. Now, here I was watching an international pop icon walking around my adopted hometown wearing it. I could not keep my eyes off Snapchat and Instagram all night long.

Needless to say, the next few days, from a social media standpoint, were really fun, and the next couple of weeks, from a sales standpoint, were off the charts. Gaga was about to drop her new album and had announced a month earlier that she would be headlining the Super Bowl LI halftime show. She was on a massive promotional campaign, so we were getting all this residual publicity from her tailwinds. It was already one of our most popular shirts, but after Lady Gaga wore it, people would come into the store every day and say, "I want the Gaga shirt." It was the middle of October at that point, so Gaga fans were purchasing the shirt to wear (along with a pink cowboy hat and short shorts) to Halloween parties all over the country.

Since then, it has become our number one bestseller, with over twelve thousand sold as of this writing, as well as our company motto and a call to action for anyone seeking to do good in the world. It's crazy that what's become an iconic phrase in a country music city was actually inspired by my love for a hip-hop song. That phrase was rolling around in my mind for years. Then you mix that up with God's plan and it has taken on a life of its own.

I've always felt that Instagram has been the best source of affirmation. As a business owner, when people post wearing our shirts, it reassures us that we should keep doing what we're doing because people are responding to our designs and our mission. On a personal level, it gives me this crazy energy that inspires me to get to the next level.

From the very beginning of this journey, the most beautiful part about starting a company like ours (and a huge part of how we define our success) is that our customers and our fans are constantly cheering us on. We've had a lot of people who have been around since day one that have been so vocal in their support of Project 615. They tell us they believe in what we're doing and to keep up the great work. We owe a ton of credit to our customers, fans, and supporters for loving on us and always encouraging us. Their purchases keep us in business and allow us to impact the world in a positive way, but their encouragement and support over the years is what inspires us to keep moving forward.

CHAPTER 8

Consider Others First

"The meeting of preparation with opportunity generates the offspring we call luck."

—TONY ROBBINS

The summer of 2016 would mark the six-year anniversary of our life-changing trip to Skid Row and our partnership with Set Free. To commemorate the occasion and celebrate our journey, we decided to launch a campaign that honored those who "Consider Others First" and donate all the proceeds back to the Set Free ministry. With this campaign we wanted to send the message that the true heroes in the world are those who work daily to serve others and transform people's lives. We wanted to spread this message beyond Nashville, and even Tennessee, and connect with our fans and customers all over the country. What better way to do that than to take Project 615 on a cross-country road trip in a vintage 1978 VW bus?

For years, Matt and I had been kicking around the idea of buying a VW bus and turning it into a mobile store and mascot for the brand. Finding one we could afford, and that we didn't have to restore ourselves practically from scratch, turned out to be a challenge. At the beginning of that summer, after years of searching with no luck, we finally found one on eBay that was in great condition and we decided to go for it. The only catch was that they guy selling the bus was in Los Angeles and it was going to cost a couple thousand dollars to have it transported to Nashville. Then we realized: Why not fly out to California to pick it up ourselves? We could drive it back to Nashville, connect with our fans and our customers along the way, and make a fun road trip out of it. Since the timing also coincided with the launch of the "Consider Others First" campaign, we decided to make honoring those who spend their lives serving others the theme of the trip.

We invited two of our buddies to join us and arranged to meet the seller at the airport in Los Angeles. We landed at LAX on June 30 and, when the seller handed over the keys, we became the proud owners of a beautifully restored, vintage 1978 Volkswagen bus. Of course, Matt and I couldn't return to Los Angeles without visiting the place where the dream of

PROJECT 615 SUMMER ROAD TRIP

Project 615 was first conceived, so the first stop on our road trip was the Set Free church in Skid Row. We had been back a few times since that first trip back in 2010, but this moment was especially meaningful for us because it coincided with our six-year anniversary. We ministered to the homeless, told the story of the business, handed out shirts, and spread the message of the "Consider Others First" campaign. Then we hit the road.

Dolly in Memphis on the tail end of our Consider Others First road trip.

Over the next five days, we drove two thousand miles along the famed Route 66 all the way back to Nashville. Along the way, we were posting about the trip to raise awareness and get the word out about the campaign, and people were leaving comments asking us to stop in their hometowns and suggesting nicknames for the bus. Going in, we knew that we wanted to stop in Las Vegas and visit the Grand Canyon, but for the most part, the trip was spontaneous and unplanned. So much so, in fact, that we accidentally ended up having to sleep in the bus two nights in a row. You take four grown men, who haven't showered for days, spending ten to twelve hours a day cooped up together inside a seven-seater VW bus, and it definitely got a little ripe in there by day three. But we were having the time of our lives.

We stopped in small towns in Nevada, Arizona, New Mexico, Texas, and Oklahoma and talked to people from all walks of life across this beautiful nation. We gave shirts to policemen, waitresses at diners, homeless people, and other road trippers. We just wanted to spread the love to others and cast the message of the campaign. It was an incredible opportunity for us, not only to tell the story of Project 615 and our partnership with Set Free, but also to spread the message that true joy and fulfillment in life comes when we strive to consider others first. When we encountered individuals who dedicate their lives to serving others, like the brave men of the Oklahoma City Fire Department, we gave them "Consider Others First" shirts as a token of our appreciation and highlighted their stories on our social media.

By the time we got back to Nashville, we knew there was only one name for the newest member of the Project 615 family: Dolly. What better way to honor the city we call home than to name our beloved VW bus after the queen of country music? To shine a light on the incredible talent that exists in Nashville, we came up with the idea of the 615 Bus Sessions and began inviting local artists and bands to hop on the bus and perform acoustic sessions of their original music. Since that summer, Dolly has become an iconic presence in Nashville. Whether she's parked outside one of our retail stores, representing the company at pop-ups, or driving through the streets of Music City, she brings a smile to everyone who sees her.

After a whirlwind summer and epic road trip, it was time to start strategizing and planning our campaigns and goals for the year ahead. Matt and I decided what we needed to get our creative juices flowing was to take the Project 615 team on a three-day brainstorming retreat. The idea was to hole up in a cabin for a few days, drink some beers, cook some good food, and immerse ourselves in work. It was an extension of the late-night creative sessions Matt and I used to have during those early years when it was just the two of us hashing out ideas on a double-sided whiteboard. It's how we've always been able to get creative and set goals. We invited Josh (our college buddy, who had hooked me up with a place to live when I first moved to Nashville) to come along as an IT consultant. Over the years, once in a while, we'd buy him dinner and he'd pop into the office for a few hours so we could pick his brain and bounce ideas off him. In addition to being a really smart guy who cares deeply about our company and our mission, his corporate experience and business savvy have been invaluable to us.

The plan was to rent a cabin at the end of November in Gatlinburg, Tennessee, a mountain resort city that sits at the gateway to the Great Smoky Mountains National Park. But, on the day after Thanksgiving, a fire broke out on the Chimney Tops trail. What began as a contained one-acre fire near the summit, rapidly spread across the entire mountain, as record-breaking eighty-seven-miles-per-hour-winds downed flaming trees onto power lines and drove sparks across the area for miles. As we watched the story unfolding on the news, it became clear that we could no longer take the team to Gatlinburg. We didn't want to cancel the retreat, so instead, we decided to rent a cabin in Cookeville, a little town tucked within the Upper Cumberland region about an hour outside of Nashville.

On day three of the fire, Matt floated the idea of putting out a Gatlinburg T-shirt to raise money for the people who were being displaced by the fire. I was a little hesitant because the timing was so close to a tragic accident in Chattanooga, about a hundred miles south of Nashville. Just a few days earlier, six elementary school children had been killed when their bus driver lost control of the wheel and crashed into a tree. It was a tragedy that had rocked the entire state and I was worried that, if we came out with a Gatlinburg tee, our customers and followers might feel we weren't supporting the Chattanooga victims. Then Gatlinburg got worse. By the time we arrived at the cabin in Cookeville, reports were coming in that over a dozen people had died in the fire, and they were estimating that more than 2,500 homes and businesses had been damaged or destroyed.

On the morning of December 1, I woke up at around 5:00 a.m. to an explosion of tweets, emails, direct messages, and comments from our followers, local media outlets, and news personalities:

"Hey, Project 615. Where's the fundraising shirt?"

"Hey, guys. Checking in to see if you have a Gatlinburg shirt."

"You guys should come out with a Gatlinburg shirt!"

"Where's the Gatlinburg shirt?!"

If you live in Tennessee, there's a good chance you go to Gatlinburg at least once a year. It's not a little mountain town that nobody's heard of. It's a vibrant, bustling city, full of res-taurants and shops, where a lot of Southern people own second homes or go on vacation. I even knew people back in Indiana who regularly rented cabins there in the winter. People all over the region were reaching out to us because they wanted to help the people of Gatlinburg and they wanted to use our platform to do it. I realized that, if this many of our fans and customers were requesting a Gatlinburg campaign, we needed to respond and launch a shirt as quickly as possible.

The sun wasn't even up yet, but I knocked on Matt's door and said, "Dude, we have to do a Gatlinburg shirt." He was a little groggy and needed a beat to catch up but as soon as I showed him all the messages we'd gotten overnight, he was all in. That was the first time that our customers reached out and essentially said, "We need Project 615 to come through for us." It was this incredibly beautiful shift, where people were now *expecting* us to respond in times of crisis and provide them an opportunity to help others. What a crazy feeling. We had a vision of building a business for change and now our customers were demanding this. It gave us more passion to want to make change in the world.

Twenty minutes later, Josh pulled up to the cabin and the three of us decided to go for a hike in the woods to clear our heads and map out a plan for how we were going to launch this shirt. There are so many factors—from design to launch—that go into planning a campaign and normally, we would spend weeks planning the execution. In this case, however, we were responding to a tragedy as it was still unfolding. We needed to get a shirt out immediately, while people were still tied to the story. If we waited two weeks to launch, people would have either have moved on or given their money elsewhere. So we decided to set aside, for the moment, the issue of selecting and vetting a legitimate nonprofit to partner with, and first tackle the design and launch announcement. First and foremost, the shirt has to resonate with people and align with the mission of the campaign. From a creative standpoint, we try to keep it simple and fairly unisex so that anybody can wear it. We usually like to incorporate some verbiage that reflects the message we are trying to convey and when we announce the launch, we want to make it clear to our customers where the money is going and what it's doing.

There's always a sense of excitement when we begin planning a campaign, and this one was no exception. It was 6:30 in the morning and we were deep in the woods, but we were so fired up, we barely noticed our surroundings. We were passionately bouncing ideas off each another, bantering, jumping up and down, and being playful. Then, all of a sudden, we heard this booming voice from above.

"Shut the hell up or I'll shoot you!"

We looked up. Directly above us, there was a guy with a rifle crouching in a tree stand. We had been so deeply engrossed in our planning that we had accidentally wandered into deer hunting territory. We decided to move our strategy session out of the woods and (very quietly) high-tailed it out of rifle range.

Back in the safety of the cabin, we began researching nonprofits and drafting a launch announcement, while Matt got to work on designing a graphic for the shirt. We had tossed around a couple of ideas on our hike, but nothing had really clicked yet. There was a little loft area in the cabin, so Matt went up there with his laptop to do his thing. On the bed, directly in front of where he was sitting, there was a little decorative pillow with a black bear and some hearts on it. For at least an hour he was staring at this pillow, wracking his brain for an idea for the design. Suddenly, a light bulb went off and he realized the answer had literally been staring him in the face. He came back down from the loft with a truly inspired design that incorporated the outline of that bear into a cool graphic that captured the essence of the Smoky Mountains. We added the verbiage "Heart for the Smokies," slapped it on a mock-up, and launched it immediately with a simple announcement explaining that 100 percent of the profits would go directly to the families who had been impacted by the wildfires.

Normally, we would have already had a nonprofit partner in place long before we actually released a shirt. By that point, we were getting requests from nonprofits weekly to partner on campaigns with us. We always vet our partners carefully, so that we know they are legit, that they have integrity, and that the money we give them is going directly to people in need. However, because we were trying to get this shirt out to our customers as quickly as possible, we decided to go ahead with the launch first while we simultaneously searched for the right nonprofit to partner with. Thankfully, within a day or two, were able to partner with the Gatlinburg Relief Fund, which was established by the Gatlinburg Chamber of Commerce Foundation, so we knew the money we donated would be going directly to help those impacted by the fire.

As soon as we went live with the "Heart for the Smokies" tee on our website, people went crazy. Almost immediately, we started getting hundreds and hundreds of shares and tags on social media. News channels and online media outlets were reposting our launch announcement on their platforms. We thought we were going to sell five hundred shirts, tops, for the whole campaign, but we ended up selling that many in the first two hours alone. By the end of that first day, the campaign had gone viral and we had raised over $20,000. That was great news for the campaign, but it caused a cascade of issues that turned into a logistical nightmare back at the print shop.

Even working around the clock, it would take our printers at least a week to produce half the shirts we had already sold. Once you factored in processing and shipping time, from day one, we were already back-ordered for a couple of weeks. Our whole goal-planning retreat came to a screeching halt and it was all hands on deck preparing to execute a campaign of this magnitude. We called another screen printer in Nashville and brought them on to handle some of the overflow printing and shipping for us. By the time we got back to town the next day, the order numbers had doubled. We had nowhere near enough blank shirts in stock to keep up with the demand, so we contacted our supplier in Cincinnati and maxed out our credit cards ordering thousands more (which would take one to two business days to arrive).

Once the campaign went viral, we started getting calls from news outlets all over the state and the region—we were even getting national media attention. At the time, my personal cell phone was (and still is—whoops) linked to the business, and for the next few weeks, it was ringing nonstop. A news channel back in Indiana even contacted me for an interview and ran a story about the "Indy native" who created a benefit T-shirt for Gatlinburg fire victims. After we were on the national news, I started getting calls from eighty-something-year-old ladies asking where they could purchase the Gatlinburg T-shirt they had seen on the television. That happened at least a half a dozen times and, after the second or third call, I realized there was no point trying to explain that we had a website (or how to use the Internet). I just gave them our address so they could send a check (and, in one case, cash) and personally handled their orders myself.

Day three is when things really got crazy. I was just starting to feel like we had a handle on the campaign. Yes, we were back-ordered for at least a couple of weeks. Yes, our little operation was being pushed to the limit of our capacity. But the Project 615 Team was rising to the challenge. The company we had subcontracted to help us with the overflow had a much larger space and more equipment, so we temporarily moved our base of operations from the church basement to their warehouse. We had every screen printer at our disposal working around the clock, but we were desperately shorthanded for shipping. So we invited all the guys from Set Free to come work for us and offered thirteen dollars an hour to help us pack and ship. In those first few days, we had already raised tens of thousands of dollars for the victims of the fire and, with the holiday shopping season just beginning to pick up steam, we were ready for whatever the next few weeks would bring—or so I thought.

That night, I was over at Matt's house. We were talking about the campaign, going over how many shirts we'd sold and discussing strategies for fulfilling all the orders still coming in, when I noticed a friend had tagged us on Twitter:

"Hey, you might want to check this out. It looks like somebody stole your Gatlinburg T-shirt design and is selling it on another website."

We clicked the link and it took us to a landing page where someone had mocked up, in several different colors, an exact copy of the "Heart for the Smokies" design that I had just watched Matt create 72 hours earlier. There was no question that it was our design; they had even ripped off the Project 615 brand logo at the bottom of the graphic. Matt and I looked at each other in total shock and disbelief.

I started looking into our accounts and quickly discovered that they had been going into our posts and replying to our customers' comments with a link to their bogus website. They were using our verbiage, so it seemed to anyone looking at the thread that this was how you could purchase our shirt. Our customers were being tricked into buying a knock-off, thinking their money was going to the Gatlinburg Relief Fund. The campaign had gone viral, so hundreds and hundreds of people were sharing our post every day, and we had to go in and delete all of the links they had embedded in these threads. I did some digging and found out that this is actually a fairly common e-commerce scam. It's not unlike knocking off Versace, Gucci, or Supreme—except, in this case, the scammers are shamelessly profiting from tragedies.

We tried to report them but unfortunately, it looked to be an overseas company (we still don't know who it was) and there wasn't much we could do to shut them down. We communicated to our customers and our followers that there was another company impersonating us and, to ensure that their purchase dollars were going to the Gatlinburg Relief Fund, they should only buy the shirt from the official Project 615 website. As the week went on, I started to relax a little. I thought: Okay, that wasn't *so* terrible. So some company tried to rip us off? We were handling it. I felt awful that some of our customers had fallen for the scam, but on the other hand, we had sold thousands of shirts and raised a lot of money for the people of Gatlinburg.

As this was going on, I was still fielding calls from the media. I had done dozens of interviews and given quotes to reporters from all over the country. Up to then, all of the press had been great. When I mentioned the scam to one of the news channels that was running a feature on the campaign, they asked if they could include it in the story to warn people about the bogus website and get the word out to only buy the shirt from the official Project 615 website. They ran the piece the next day and the story was great; everything that was written was factual and correct. However, they ran the article with the headline "Gatlinburg T-shirt Scam" next to a photo of *our* design on our model with our official logo. To make matters worse, it wasn't just one local channel that ran the story; all of their affiliates picked it up as well. So we had news channels from St. Louis to Tuscaloosa publishing that headline next to our shirt.

Most people didn't click on or read the actual article; they just saw the headline—and, when people see something online, they believe it's true. As quickly as the campaign had gone viral in one direction, the pendulum now swung in the other and a rumor rapidly began to spread that Project 615 was behind the T-shirt scam. Suddenly, the comments on our social media went from applauding the work we were doing, to people asking if *we* were the scammers. My phone started blowing up with calls from confused customers demanding their money back. It was a disaster that went beyond just the campaign. This was a potentially catastrophic rumor that could undermine our customers' faith in our core mission.

I called every single news outlet that ran the story and explained how damaging the headline was. Very quickly, it was corrected to "Project 615 Investigates T-shirt Scam" but, by then, the rumor had gotten enough traction that people were still confused. We released an official statement, explaining that Project 615 is a legitimate social enterprise and that we were, in fact, giving 100 percent of the profits from this campaign to the Gatlinburg Relief Fund. I had to do a lot of cleanup, and we definitely lost some sales, but the issue for us wasn't the campaign, which was already a success by any measure. The real problem was that the reputation of our company and the Project 615 brand had gotten tangled up in misinformation.

As the president and co-founder of a philanthropic business, it was a PR nightmare. As a human being who believes passionately that the work he is doing is having a positive impact on the world, it was a devastating blow. It took hundreds of one-to-one phone calls with our customers and a whole lot of copying and pasting of our official statement into customer service emails (I felt like Wile E. Coyote chasing the Road Runner...never ending), but thankfully our fans and customers rallied around us and we were able to squash the rumor almost as quickly as it reared its ugly head.

Meanwhile, even as I was dealing with all that insanity, we were still selling hundreds of shirts a day. A lot of people were ordering for Christmas, so two weeks into the campaign, it became a race against the clock to get them shipped out to our customers in time. But it seemed like every time I turned around, there was some new crisis at the warehouse. Most of the guys we had brought in from Set Free to help out with the shipping were great, but there were a couple who either didn't pay attention (or didn't care) who were literally just slapping labels on any shipment. So suddenly, we were getting emails from Jill in St. Louis, wondering where her size medium Gatlinburg T-shirt was. Well, it turned out that it had gone to Mark in Canada, and his size XL had been shipped to Elaine in Dallas—and so on, and so on. There were probably five or six hundred orders that were labeled incorrectly, so on top of everything else, we were now dealing with hundreds of returns.

I take every single customer service inquiry to heart—and when there's a thousand of them coming at you all at once, it takes over your life. I was working sixteen- to eighteen-hour days, every single day, for weeks. We were determined to maintain the quality of our product and our standard of service, even as we were scrambling to adapt to the success of the campaign and troubleshoot all the issues that come with rapid growth. You're not going to go from raising a few thousand here and there to a six-figure campaign and have things be business as usual. Along with growth comes all kinds of issues, and you have to be ready to respond and adapt.

We were so determined to fulfill every order that on Christmas Eve we went out in our own cars and personally delivered orders all over Tennessee. By January, we had raised over $102,000. Then we extended the campaign into February and raised an additional $6,000—a donation that went directly to the Gatlinburg Relief Fund to assist sixty businesses and hundreds of their employees whose buildings and homes were destroyed by the wildfires by providing housing, food, clothing, and funds to pay urgent bills. After all the ups and downs throughout that campaign, it was gratifying to know that all of our hard work and dedication had been worth it.

As an entrepreneur committed to this type of business of serving people, I learned that there will be times when it is going to be insane. Your phone is going to ring all night long. You're going to have well-meaning old ladies trying to mail you cash for your product. Your reputation may even be dragged through the mud, and you're going to look in the mirror and ask yourself: *Why? Why did I choose this path? Is it worth it?* If your answer to the last question is "yes," then this kind of work is for you. I think that's the lesson in any business. It's constant work, but when that work is about changing the world, the success and the victories are measured by the impact you have on other people's lives.

CHAPTER 9

Live for Today

"Today you are You,
that is truer than true.
There is no one alive
who is Youer than You."

—DR. SEUSS

Project 615 has always been more than just a T-shirt brand. First and foremost, we are a social enterprise on a mission to transform people's lives and change the world, but we are also a company that our customers are drawn to because of the fun and youthful joy for life that is at the core of everything we do. Matt and I had brought that spirit to Project 615 from our early days dreaming up funny T-shirt ideas for Huggable Tees.

The business was born out of a brotherhood that began with laughter and evolved into a vision of changing the world. The beautiful community of followers and fans that had unexpectedly sprung up around us, both locally in Nashville and globally through social media, connected with that energy as much as our mission.

Something we have always tried to do with the Project 615 brand is celebrate the glorious city of Nashville. A big part of growing as a business is branching into different markets and taking risks, so, in addition to our nonprofit campaigns and our positive messaging and country-music-themed shirts, we began designing a line of tees and accessories inspired by Music City's beloved athletic teams. Sports are a big deal in this town, especially hockey and football, so we tapped into the creative wellspring that had made the Cannonball Creative brand so appealing to the youth athletic market and created designs with a sense of humor that Nashville fans could wear to rep their team pride.

In early 2017, we were approached by the Nashville Predators' Pro Shop about including some of our designs in the store at Bridgestone Arena. We met with one of their reps, who picked out a few of our hockey-inspired shirts and ordered 144 pieces of each—including our "Fang Fingers" and "Catfish" designs that were a nod to Preds fans' tradition of taunting the opposing team during power plays. During the meeting, we asked if we could market the shirts as an official partnership with the Predators. He was just a young kid working in the Pro Shop, but he put us in touch with the Corporate Partnerships department and we ended up becoming an official sponsor with our company name and logo on the plexiglass above the boards at Bridgestone Arena. Any time you can partner with a professional sports team is huge—especially for a small business like ours—and it couldn't have come at a better time because we were about be thrust from our rent-free haven in the church basement into the harsh reality of searching for a new headquarters at the peak of Nashville's commercial real estate market.

In January of that year, we had got word that the landlord was putting all the buildings he'd been renting to Set Free on the market, including the church, and I realized that we needed to start looking for a new home immediately. When you're a company that operates out of the basement of an abandoned church (that you share with a nonprofit homeless ministry), your overhead is minimal. For the past seven years, that had allowed us the financial freedom to focus on giving back to Set Free and all the other nonprofits we had partnered with. On the other hand, because we weren't officially on the lease, the reality was that we could be out on the street any minute. We really had nothing to hold us in place. We had snuck in years ago, and the landlord had allowed us to stay, but we had always known it was inevitable that some day he would sell the buildings and we would have to move.

We started putting out feelers and by March, we had looked at five or six warehouse spaces all over the city. They were all obviously a huge jump for us in terms of overhead, but a couple were within a budget we felt we could support. Then we got a call from some friends of ours in the social enterprise community. ABLE is an ethical fashion brand whose mission is to end generational poverty by providing economic opportunities for women around the world. They had just moved into a new space in The Nations, an up-and-coming neighborhood in West Nashville. They knew of a warehouse space near their new location and suggested we talk to the landlord.

Matt and I drove over to the west side of town to check it out. At 8,000 square feet, not only was it way more space than we were initially looking for, it was also by far the most expensive location we had seen. We were ready to walk away and move into one of the other spaces, but the landlord pursued us. At the time, The Nations was in the midst of a transformation from a largely industrial neighborhood, filled with lumberyards and auto body shops, to a trendy retail hub. The landlord had a vision of this area of town becoming something truly special and was looking for locally owned, ethical businesses like ours to move into his properties. We loved the neighborhood and we definitely wanted to part of a community of like-minded business owners, but once again, we found ourselves at a cross-roads where the company's growth required a financial leap of faith on our part—which was terrifying.

If there was one thing we had learned from our struggles with the "Heart for the Smokies" campaign the previous year, it was that, in order to keep being a company that helps others, we needed to grow. The success of that campaign was an incredible validation of our core mission, but at the same time, it also shined a spotlight on the limitations of our infrastructure. We had been caught completely off-guard and at that point, we just didn't have the staff or the equipment to handle the orders that were coming in. As a social enterprise, doing good is the core of our business, not just something that happens along the way, and for companies like ours that have a business model tied to a social mission, growth is a means to achieving a greater impact in the world. If we wanted to continue to be the kind of company that could respond to tragedies in real time, we needed to hire more staff and we needed a bigger warehouse space so we could expand our printing and shipping departments.

Opening a second store was not something we had even considered before, but in the end, we realized that the only way we could afford the rent for the space in West Nashville was if it doubled as both our headquarters and a retail location. We pitched the idea to the landlord and he loved it. Once we signed the lease, the next few weeks were a whirlwind of activity. We hired carpenters and a construction crew to begin building out the print shop, shipping and inventory warehouse, and retail space. We brought in two more printers and added a person in marketing, as well as a full-time shipping manager and additional sales staff for the second store. Almost overnight, we went from a team of twelve to a team of twenty.

To promote the new store, we began planning a grand opening. In the spirit of the launch for our first store, we wanted the event to have a block-party vibe. So we brought in food trucks, offered door prizes, and even arranged to have GNASH, the Predators' mascot, make a special appearance. The rollercoaster of emotions leading up to that day was very similar to when we opened the Fatherland store exactly one year and eleven months earlier—except this time, we weren't moving into a $495-a-month, 192-square-foot storefront. Now, we were committing to a 1,000-square-foot flagship retail space, inside an 8,000-square-foot headquarters. It was a pivotal moment for us because we had no idea if we could sustain the overhead on this location for a year, much less into the future.

On the day of the opening, I arrived at our new West Nashville location three hours early to make sure everything was in order. To my absolute amazement, there was already a crowd of people gathering outside. By the time we opened the doors at 11:00 a.m., there was a line of over two hundred people waiting to get in. We had good numbers come out for the Fatherland

Customers and fans at the grand opening of our second location on May 20th, 2017. There were over two hundred people waiting in line before we opened.

opening, but this was *huge*. It was such an incredible affirmation of support from our fans, as well as a blessing. I remember walking outside to take a photo for our social media and feeling totally overwhelmed. It moved me to tears because these were fans and customers who had supported us for so many years. By the end of the day, a couple thousand people had come through the store to show their support. It was our biggest day ever. We didn't pay for two years' worth of rent (like we did at the Fatherland opening), but we were certainly covered for the next few months at least.

Meanwhile, Nashville was in the middle of a Stanley Cup playoff run. We had kind of snuck in the back door as sponsors of the team and thankfully, we did, because that postseason ended up being one of the most exciting in Smashville's twenty-year history. In April, the Predators swept the first round of the playoffs, and by May, they had secured a spot in the finals, sparking a six-game battle for the Cup. The entire city was on fire with Stanley Cup fever. As the Predators advanced, every week we were coming out with new playoff-themed shirts. The fans went wild. Everybody wanted one. Every single day, week after week, we had a line out the door at both stores of people who were trying to get the latest and best playoff shirt. The Project 615 journey has been marked by all these moments of spectacular timing, and this one was no exception. Nobody else in town had Predators merchandise, and now our shirts were hot and cool and trending. It was a defining moment that took us to a whole new level, and we were blessed to have the team in place to handle it.

A personal highlight for me was being invited by the team to ride the Zamboni before Game 6 of the Stanley Cup Finals. I remember being backstage with Tim McGraw and Titans quarterback Marcus Mariota as Faith Hill was getting ready to sing the national anthem, and feeling so blessed to be a part of this exciting moment that had been building in Nashville for weeks. My love of sports goes all the way back to studying broadcast journalism in college. I had stepped off that path to follow my heart—not knowing where it would lead me—and now here I was riding the Zamboni before a sold-out Predators game on national television. Matt and I looked at each other, thinking: "What is this life?!" It was such an insane moment.

That year, we also undertook several nonprofit campaigns that were very dear to our hearts. Nashville is a town full of musicians, and over the years, we've been fortunate to build relationships with a lot of up-and-coming artists and bands. Early on, we sparked a dialogue with then-rising country music singer Thomas Rhett, who from time to time would shout us out on social media for the work we were doing to improve the lives of orphans around the world. That conversation evolved into a formal partnership and, inspired by the yearlong journey he and his wife, Lauren, had undertaken to adopt their daughter, Willa, from an orphanage in Uganda, we agreed that orphan care should be the focus of our campaign. Working closely with TR and Lauren on the design, we created a limited-edition tee that incorporated his "Home Team" slogan (a phrase he uses to celebrate his fans) and the Tennessee Tri-Star, with 100 percent of the profits going to 147 Million Orphans, a local nonprofit organization that provided critical needs to orphans living in abject poverty around the world.* We released it to coincide with his sold-out concert in Nashville that April.

Over the years, we have been blessed by a lot of celebrity attention. Their support of our core mission has helped to

---

*147 Million Orphans has since transitioned into "Love One International." For more information, visit loveoneinternational.org.

The Project 615 team with Thomas Rhett and his wife, Lauren. The Home Team Campaign raised over $60,000 to aid orphans around the world.

elevate our brand and further our goal of changing the world, but what was particularly exciting about this relationship was working with TR during his very first headline tour, as he cemented himself as one of country music's superstars. He had been on a sharp upward trajectory since the release of his global hit "Die a Happy Man," which earned him multiple award wins at the CMAs, ACMs, Billboard Music Awards, and others. And, just three weeks prior to his two sold-out shows at Nashville's Ascend Amphitheater, he took home the 2017 ACM Awards for "Male Vocalist of the Year" and "Song of the Year." You couldn't have asked for better timing for the campaign. We raised over $60,000 for 147 Million Orphans, which provided three daily meals to residents of a school and children's home in Uganda for nearly a full year.

That summer was a period of tremendous growth for Project 615. Between the Home Team campaign and the playoff run, we had our hands full at both retail locations, not to mention all the products we were printing and shipping out every week to customers all over the world. It was such a blessing—and very much needed, financially speaking, because our overhead had just gone up exponentially. We were so busy, in fact, that we barely had time to process all the changes going on internally. On the day we moved out of the church, Matt and I were running at a hundred miles an hour, trying to keep up with the growth that was happening, so we didn't have a moment to process all we had been through. There was no time to stop and reflect on the move and all that we had accomplished in that church basement. Our new headquarters were such an upgrade that it was hard to feel nostalgic about leaving that cramped and dingy basement. It was like when you buy a new pair of shoes and they look and feel so much better you realize: How in the world was I walking around all that time in my old pair?

There was a little bit of sadness when we moved, but it really sunk in when we found out that Set Free was moving to a new location a few miles north and the old buildings were going to be torn down. Towards the end of that summer, Matt and I went back to visit our old headquarters. I remember walking through the building all those months later and reminiscing about old times. We talked about all the different guys who had worked for us (the ones who had gone on to rebuild their lives and those we had lost to their demons). We laughed as we remembered the day the termites invaded the inventory room. For the last time, we took the narrow flight of steps down to the basement, which was once again dark and empty, and recalled that first day Matt and I snuck into the church and realized we could turn it into our headquarters.

It was incredible to think how much had changed since that day. We had grown from a two-man operation in a vermin-infested basement of an abandoned church located in the heart of the projects into a successful social impact company with two retail locations and a headquarters in one of Nashville's fastest-growing neighborhoods. As we said goodbye to our old headquarters, I can't say we were nostalgic for the days of dealing with rats and termites, but we were eternally grateful that God had led us to Set Free and the building that been instrumental in the realization of our vision for Project 615. It was awesome to see how, when God speaks, it's truth and you should be obedient to that calling. It was an awesome ride.

As that summer came to an end, we embarked on a campaign that would remind us how precious life is, and that we must strive every moment of every day to be our best selves. A friend of mine had sent me a viral video of former Tennessee Titans linebacker Tim Shaw speaking at Nashville's Crosspoint Church about his experience living with ALS, a devastating neurological disease that systematically weakens muscles in the body, stealing a person's ability to walk, talk, and eventually breathe, as it progresses. After an inspiring introduction from the pastor, Tim took the stage and spoke of how his identity, for many years, was not found in his faith, but in his life as a football player. After his diagnosis, he began to examine his life and came to the realization that neither the NFL nor ALS define him as a person. He decided that from that moment on, he would live the rest of his life to the fullest and strive to find joy in helping others.

I was deeply moved by Tim's words, but what got my wheels turning about partnering with him on a campaign was that he was wearing our "Spread Love" shirt while he delivered this inspiring message. I couldn't stop thinking about how cool it would be to partner with this amazing man and do something for those suffering from ALS in Tennessee. Our mission and Tim's mission were so closely aligned, it was a perfect marriage. We reached out to him and made plans to launch a campaign to raise money and support for the ALS Association Tennessee Chapter, which works tirelessly to give those suffering with the disease and their families the hands-on love and support they need.

The "Live for Today" campaign was inspired by Tim's unflinching determination to live each day with purpose and intention. Following his diagnosis, rather than give in to despair, he authored a book and traveled all over the world (including a journey of service to the Amazon jungle to help an impoverished village dig a freshwater well and a mission trip to Haiti to assist orphanage workers). Despite his slurred speech and deteriorating motor function, he delivered speeches at churches and universities all over the country to raise awareness for the battle against ALS and inspire others to do good in the world. To celebrate Tim's life and message of positivity, we designed two limited-edition "Live for Today" tees, one in white and another in Titans navy and light blue, and launched the campaign to coincide with the Walk to Defeat ALS in Nashville that September.

That same month, Tim was made an honorary captain by his teammates, and Coach Mike Mularkey surprised the entire Titans team and staff with "Live for Today" tees. It was such a thrill to see some of the guys wearing our shirts during warm-ups. The campaign raised over $20,000 that went directly to the ALS Association Tennessee Chapter, and provided everything from equipment rentals, to support groups, to in-home visits.

I think Coach Mularkey truly captured the spirit of the campaign when he defined living for today as "being intentional, both in your words and through your actions. It means staying in the moment and appreciating every opportunity directly in front of you, even ones that produce adversity. It is

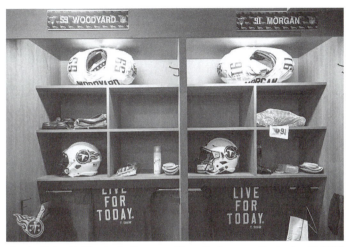

Live for Today T-shirts in the Tennessee Titans' locker room. September 10, 2017.

serving others, showing gratitude, and staying in the present, neither obsessing on the past nor looking ahead to the future. It is being all in, right here, right now." Spending time with Tim, being in his presence and having the opportunity to see first-hand his joyful approach to life, was a much-needed reminder that every breath we take is a blessing from God.

For me, living for today meant momentarily stepping away from the business to travel and refuel my soul. I had always wanted to go to Ireland, so instead of allowing life's excuses to continue standing in my way, I just got up and booked a flight to Dublin and went by myself. It was such a beautiful trip for me, personally and spiritually. It shouldn't take being diagnosed with a terminal illness to do the things you've always wanted to do or be the person you've always wanted to be. I came back from Ireland energized by an entrepreneurial spirit and passion to continue to build the business.

Matt also took the "Live for Today" message deeply to heart. After seven years, working at a relentless pace to build the company we had envisioned on the streets of Skid Row, he decided it was time for him to step away from Project 615. The core mission was still in his heart, but he needed to pursue his own entrepreneurial path. On his last official day in early 2018, we had a celebratory lunch at the office. I stood up in front of the entire team and talked about Huggable Tees, our cheerleading and softball days with Cannonball, the Set Free basement, our missional hires, and all the campaigns that had allowed us to directly help others and have an impact on the world.

As I ran through all these memories, my eyes began welling up to the point where I could barely see. I was so overcome that, by the end of my speech, all I could do was look over at my friend and business partner and, with tears streaming down my face, say, "Matt, we did it."—by then, he was crying too—"This mission that God called us to do, we did it. And I'm so grateful." We had begun this journey with a shared dream of a company that ended up being so much bigger and more impactful than we had even dared to imagine. It was a beautiful and emotional moment where we were agreeing that it was time for us each to begin forging a new path.

Matt and Derek.

The beautiful thing about our partnership, and a huge part of why the company became so successful, is that we always agreed on the mission of the company. That never changed. When we talk about doing work that matters, Matt and I like to use the phrase "mutual transformation." It's this incredible spiritual transaction that occurs when you think you're doing work to help others and change the world but, in fact, *you* are changed by the experience as well. When you are doing any sort of charity work, whether it's a mission trip to an orphanage in a third world country or serving the homeless in your own hometown, you are actually receiving as much (or more) than you are giving, because the gift of serving others brings joy and purpose to your life.

Serving others is not all just about the people you are helping—and sometimes it's not about them at all—it's about *you*. That was certainly the case for Matt and me when we embarked on that mission trip to Skid Row all those years ago. We had gone into it thinking that we were there to transform other people's lives, and certainly we met some physical needs by providing food and clothing. But, in truth, it was *our* lives that were changed. The moment we decided to make serving others the focus of our lives and our business, we became energized by a deeply spiritual sense of purpose that, to this day, continues to bring joy and success to our lives.

When you entwine your journey in life with a mission of serving others, without expecting anything in return, you will be rewarded tenfold by spiritual fulfillment and purpose. That is the story of my personal journey, and what I believe God has done for us. He put us on this Earth and gave us all these gifts, yet requires nothing in return. The beauty of life is that the more you serve others and the more good you put into the world, the richer your own life is going to be.

After all, *you* are made to change the world.

CHAPTER 10

You Are Made to Change the World

"If you've got nothing worth dying for, you've got nothing worth living for."

—DR. MARTIN LUTHER KING, JR.

Every great start-up business begins with a mission. For most companies, that mission is simply to provide products and services that consumers will buy. The beauty of what we have built with Project 615 is that we have been able to align our professional commitment to providing quality products with a personal commitment to our vision of a better world.

As any entrepreneur will tell you, building a successful company is a marathon, not a sprint. You need to have a strong spirit to persevere through the challenges of business. This is especially true when what you are building is a company based on a philanthropic model. It is my sincerest hope that, in sharing the story of the Project 615 journey—the highs and lows, the triumphs and the struggles, the blood, sweat, and tears—you too may be inspired to build something that changes that world.

I would like to leave you with some key points that I believe have helped me in overcoming some of the difficulties involved in creating a socially conscious business. In times when I have doubted myself or needed affirmation in my struggle to realize the Project 615 mission, I have looked to my personal heroes for inspiration. Their stories embody the principles that govern my life and work and have pushed me along on my journey.

Be the Underdog

The most important thing to remember when you set out to build something that truly changes the world is that you've got to *believe*—in yourself and in your vision. There will be haters and doubters, even family and loved ones, who will tell you that you cannot do it. You must reach deep inside of yourself and change your mentality to a place of "this *will* happen." As the great Muhammad Ali once said, "Impossible is not a fact. It's an opinion."

On a gray and windy afternoon in May 1954, one of my personal heroes, Roger Bannister, a twenty-five-year-old medical student in London, achieved something that, up to that point, was universally considered physiologically impossible. Before a modest crowd of 1,200 spectators assembled at a track meet between Oxford University and the British Amateur Athletic Association, Bannister ran a mile in three minutes and 59.4 seconds—breaking through a mystical barrier that had daunted runners for generations. It was the Mount Everest of athletic achievement.

What is so inspiring to me about this achievement isn't that Bannister was an extraordinary athlete—in fact, up until that historic moment, Bannister's story was actually pretty unremarkable. He was a solid middle-distance runner who had finished fourth at the 1952 Olympics, but by all accounts, running was more of a hobby to him. After his relative failure in Helsinki that year, he spent a couple of months deciding whether to give up the sport and focus on his medical studies. Instead, he decided to set himself a new goal: to be the first man to run a mile in under four minutes. Up to then, the four-minute barrier was considered humanly impossible to cross—many had tried, and some even came close, with no success. But Bannister was determined to break through it so that others might follow in his footsteps. And what *is* extraordinary about his story is that they *did*. Once Bannister broke the record, it changed everyone's perception of what the human body could accomplish and almost immediately after that race, other runners started breaking through the barrier as well.

Bannister's ordinary greatness is a testament to the power of the mind. It sends a beautiful message that we *all* have the capacity to turn the impossible into the possible. Not only has this idea been a powerful inspiration in my personal life, it's also the story of the Project 615 journey. It seemed impossible that two college buddies, with no money and very little business background, could build a profitable social enterprise with a mission to change the world and succeed, but that's exactly what we set out to do and it's exactly what we did.

When you're building a business, especially one with a social impact, don't place limits on your belief in it. Tell yourself a story and play that out in your mind. Your thinking needs to go from "I can't" to "I will." The *process* is where you need to live at all times. The mountaintop is an illusion; it doesn't exist. The journey of building the business is the real adventure. Along the way, things will go wrong—like, so wrong it will hurt—and you may be tempted to give up. But the truth is: Failure is just feedback. After all, the person who invented the ship also invented the shipwreck. You've got to be willing to dust yourself off when you fall. Are you willing to do that? Dig deep inside you; there's a person in there looking to flourish in life.

There's an iconic photo of Bannister—eyes closed, head thrown back in exhaustion, body pushed to the point of human endurance—that was taken at the moment he crossed the finish line. It's a portrait of human triumph that speaks volumes of one man's determination to defy convention and follow his own path. When we moved into our new headquarters in West Nashville, I had a 36-by-24-inch reproduction of this photograph mounted on the wall in my office as a reminder that once you stop believing something is impossible, it becomes possible.

Do Work That Matters

I believe the secret sauce to personal and professional fulfillment in any type of business is: *work that matters*. Most entrepreneurs are just people solving problems. The social entrepreneur is someone who sees a problem in the world and designs a business solution in response. The vision behind Project 615 began with a mission to help change the lives of homeless people in Nashville, and that grew into a larger mission of helping others around the world.

Every elementary schoolchild in America learns the story of the black seamstress who bravely refused to give up her seat to a white man on a Montgomery, Alabama, city bus on her way home from a long day at work—defying racist Jim Crow segregation laws and sparking the civil rights movement. Rosa Parks is a national treasure (one of only four private citizens—the first woman and second African-American—to lie in state after she passed away in 2005) because she decided to put a bookmark in this world with her own life and take a stand against injustice that forever changed the fabric of our society. We teach children her story so that they understand our nation's complicated history, but also to remind them that we must all strive to stand up for what's right because one seemingly small act has the power to ignite a revolution that changes the world.

As entrepreneurs, we can learn from her story as well. Either we can build companies that serve only the bottom line, or we can choose to make the work we do impact the world in a positive way. At Project 615, doing good isn't just our mission, it's our business model. We believe that doing good *is* good business. People don't buy products; they buy identity. In today's world, consumers want to be associated with brands that reflect their core values. When you create products and services that people want to get behind and stand with, you build more than a consumer base. You inspire a community of passionate supporters.

When Matt and I set out to build a company with a mission to help the homeless in our community, we could never have imagined how successful the business would become. We knew we wanted to do something impactful through our partnerships with nonprofit organizations as well as our missional hires, and we showed up every day with a work-that-matters attitude.

That is what our customers responded to. We are a brand that stands up for change and people want to be a part of that.

Once you realize that serving people is far more effective than entering a business for yourself or for selfish gain, you've got to burn your boats and live on that "island." To truly have success with a social enterprise, there's no turning back. It's about commitment to your vision. If you're not going to spend five years on it, don't spend five minutes. Be intentional and authentic, because if *you* don't care, no one else will either. Stay inspired constantly. Your own story is how your business will be successful. Be obsessed with adding value to others (the people who are benefiting from your mission, but also those who are helping you with your mission). Surround yourself with others who are also striving to change the world. Hire optimistic people who believe in the vision of how you are changing the world. If someone is there solely to collect a paycheck, they aren't there for the right reasons. I'm not saying money doesn't matter, but your team should be motivated by the mission.

I believe we should all strive to make standing up for change and doing work that matters a professional mission. Whether it's a one-for-one model, sourcing ethically produced and eco-friendly materials, or adopting an employment model that provides meaningful work to a disadvantaged population (or all three!), the opportunities for entrepreneurs to incorporate socially responsible practices into their business models are boundless. When your business focuses on purpose alongside profit, your customer loyalty will grow, and you will achieve unimaginable fulfillment and joy, as well as financial prosperity.

Utilize Your Gifts and Talents

When customers visit our East Nashville store, they are greeted by a ten-by-ten-foot print of one of my all-time favorite photographs hanging behind the register. It captures a beautiful moment from Johnny Cash's legendary 1968 performance inside Folsom State Prison, where he recorded his iconic live album, *At Folsom Prison*. The photo was taken moments after Johnny finished performing "Greystone Chapel," the final song of the show, and he is reaching down from the stage to shake hands with a man in the front row.

The man he's shaking hands with was an inmate named Glen Sherley, who was serving a three-year sentence at Folsom for armed robbery. A career criminal, Sherley had a come-to-faith transformation while in prison and began writing and recording gospel and country music songs as a refuge from the harsh realities of prison life. On the night before the concert, the prison chaplain gave Johnny a demo recording of "Greystone Chapel," an uplifting ballad about finding God in the chapel at Folsom, and he was so impressed, he decided to surprise Sherley by performing it to close the show. Cash would later become instrumental in securing Sherley's early release and was even there to meet him at the prison gate on the day he was granted his freedom.

One of the things I admire most about Johnny Cash is that he was known to be a deeply religious man, but he was also a notorious rebel. (The concert itself was an act of rebellion against his record label, which only reluctantly agreed to fund the recording.) It was the authenticity of these two sides of his nature that made his connection to the men of Folsom so powerful and the performance so inspiring—not only did the inmates see him as one of them, he saw himself in them as well. On the album, between songs, you can hear Johnny talking about drinking too much and cracking jokes about how to break out of prison. Whenever I listen to it, I'm always reminded of my grandfather, Robert Lunn, who (like Cash) was a man who walked the line between saint and sinner. Both men are among my personal heroes and I have modeled my own journey on their example. Project 615 was born out of a drive to do good, but as a social entrepreneur you also need to have that rebellious spirit. The mission of the company has always been to stand up for what's right and effect positive change in the world, but we defied convention and bent some rules along the way.

After the Folsom show, Cash continued to perform for inmates at prisons all over the country and became an outspoken advocate of prison reform. He had a passion to love on people with his music and used his God-given gifts and talents to provide hope and inspiration to members of our society that most would consider unworthy of compassion and incapable of redemption. At Project 615, we have the same mission. We are a company that strives to utilize our gifts and talents to provide hope through our missional hires and our partnerships with world-changing nonprofit organizations. We hang that photo of Johnny Cash and Glen Sherley in our store to honor all the unsung heroes who use their gifts and talents to serve the least of these and to inspire others to do the same. For me, the photo has always served as a personal reminder of what we can achieve when we begin to align our passions with a mission of helping others.

When building a vision of changing the world, it is imperative that you seek that natural talent that is inside of *you*. What desire is stirring in your heart that you feel God is speaking to you? True faith is not just assurance in a certain outcome, but rather an absolute confidence in God's unfailing character and ability, that He has, in fact, made *you* to change the world. When God speaks, He means it. What is He speaking to you? Once a quarter, take the time to be silent and still for a day or weekend. Reflect. Pray. Think. Challenge your own ideas and preconceptions. What is inside you that makes you get up in the morning? That's the thing you must find. What do other people tell you that you are good at? What have you been through? What have you already conquered? What is something that never seems to "go away" from your thoughts or dreams? You can be sixteen or ninety-six. It's never too late to begin your entrepreneurial journey. Start today.

The message behind our "Spread Love" shirt was a little seed that was planted during my childhood because of my passion for hip-hop. It took root as I sought to find my life mission and build my company and then, eventually, grew into a movement that has inspired people all around the world. What's so beautiful about that particular shirt is that people from all walks of life and persuasions have embraced its message. We've seen people wearing it everywhere from LGBTQ rallies to evangelical Christian churches. The message is so simple and true that it transcends the politics and ideologies that divide us as human beings and reminds us all that love is a universal force that can truly change the world.

Campaigns That Changed the World

2012

Take Action Send Love—Our very first campaign, which raised a little over $3,000 to bring Christmas joy to orphans in Haiti.

Set Free Nashville received a $5,000 donation to help those recovering from homelessness, addiction, and mental illness.

2013

Hope for ALL & A Home for One—raised $500 for Show Hope Ministries, which helps connect orphans to adopted families.

Freedom Is Beautiful—Partnered with Project Hope, whose mission is to end human sex trafficking in Southern California, to raise money and awareness for their organization.

Love Big—Raised money to help a Nashville family cover the medical and adoption costs of a five-year-old with special needs from China.

2014

Tri-Star Africa—In partnership with Sweet Sleep, raised $13,000 to bring Christmas joy to orphans in Ethiopia.

Blood:Water—In partnership with Blood Water Mission, built a fresh water well in Uganda.

Set Free Nashville received a $5,000 donation to help those recovering from homelessness, addiction, and mental illness.

2015

$20,000 donated to help those recovering from homelessness, addiction, and mental illness.

Heart for the Hungry—1,000 meals donated to the Bridge Ministry to aid in the fight against hunger.

Freedom Is Everything—Donated $3,500 to ONEless Ministries to help in their fight to end human trafficking in Tennessee.

Nashville Stands With Paris—$2,000 given in aid after the Paris attacks.

2016

Named a finalist by *USA Today* and *The Tennessean* for a "Your Town" Award for our work helping rehabilitate the homeless in Nashville.

Heart for the Smokies—Raised more $108,000 for the Gatlinburg Relief Fund to support families who lost sources of income, businesses, and homes in the wildfires in East Tennessee and the Great Smoky Mountains region.

Consider Others First—Donated $4,000 to Set Free Nashville to go towards housing those who are recovering from homelessness, addiction, and mental illness.

Heart for the Hungry—Donated 1,000 meals to the Bridge Ministry to feed children in need in honor of Child Hunger Day.

2017

Over $113,000 given to world-changing causes, including:

Live for Today—In partnership with Titans captain Tim Shaw, raised $21,130 for the ALS Association Tennessee Chapter to support, advocate for, and empower those affected by ALS to live their lives to the fullest, while working to find treatments and a cure.

Today Is the Day to Be Kind—In partnership with the Music City Cares Fund, raised $6,000 for those affected by the mass shooting in Las Vegas.

Pray for Texas—$5,000 donation to Global Living's Hurricane Harvey Relief Fund to provide critical aid to those affected by the devastating hurricane in Texas and along the Gulf Coast in the form of food, water, and medicine, as well as long-term assistance to help residents recover and rebuild.

Home Team—In partnership with country music star Thomas Rhett, raised $61,603 to benefit 147 Million Orphans, a non-profit that provides critical needs to international orphans living in abject poverty.

Heart for the Hungry—1,257 meals donated to the Bridge Ministry for children suffering from hunger in Middle Tennessee.

Love Your Neighbor—raised $10,000 for local homeless shelter Room in the Inn to help rehabilitate those recovering from homelessness in Nashville.

2018–2019

Over $160,000 donated to world-changing causes, including:

Love People & Do Good—In partnership with the Bridge Ministry, raised the equivalent of thirty-eight thousand meals for homeless families in Nashville.

Be the Change—Raised $5,000 for the Shine Project Scholarship Fund, a 501(c)(3) that is committed to empowering youth through providing jobs, mentoring, college scholarships, and a positive community for inner-city youth in Nashville.

Do Everything in Love—In partnership with Project R12, raised $25,000 and built a children's home in Uganda.

Waffle House/Spread Love Sign—Raised $44,242 to support the immediate and long-term needs of the victims and families of the Waffle House shooting in Nashville.

Unfinished Business—In partnership with Nashville Predators veteran Mike Fisher, this limited-edition T-shirt that was exclusively sold throughout the 2018 playoffs raised $12,000 for the Nashville Predators Foundation, a nonprofit organization that works to improve the lives of youths and their families in Middle Tennessee.

35 for 35—In partnership with the Predators Foundation and Preds goaltender Pekka Rinne (#35), raised $21,600 in 35 days for the 365 Pediatric Cancer Fund.

Made to Change the World—Raised $15,482 for the nonprofit People Loving Nashville as they work to feed, clothe, and serve the homeless in Nashville. Every Monday night for the last ten years, rain or shine, the hard-working leaders within this nonprofit organization have prepared home-cooked meals, gathered clothing and sought fellowship with those in need at War Memorial Plaza in the heart of Nashville. The funds raised through this campaign provided nearly thirty-five weeks worth of these life-changing services to a community in need.

ACKNOWLEDGMENTS

To my mom and dad. Thank you so much for showing me great love and pointing us kids in the right direction. I love you both very much! Thank you for showing me hard work and teaching me to do the right thing.

To my wonderful and beautiful wife, Mary. I love you very much. Thank you for being a Godly woman and always loving me. Without your love, encouragement, and prayers, none of this is possible! I'm so glad for our story!

To my wonderful sister, Erin. I love you very much. You are funny, witty, and smart. You are a great mother who has great strength. Thanks for putting up with me and choosing to still love me after all those wild childhood years.

To my awesome brother, Trevor. Love you, bro! You are funny, patient, and loyal. You have been a constant in my life since day one. Thanks for always supporting, encouraging, and loving me. I couldn't ask for a better brother!

To all current and former Project 615 team: Thank you all for believing in this mission and vision of changing the world. Thanks for believing in "work that matters." Every single one of you helped move the needle of world change. I am forever grateful for all your hard work, passion, creativity, energy, drive, strength, and compassion.

To my business partner, Matt Blinco: Out of the 1,000 people that I talked to about my dream of starting a business, you were the one to support me and say, "Let's do it!" Who would have thought that God would choose us to take this awesome journey together? You are strong, patient, trustworthy, smart, dependable, and creative. Thanks for all the many long road trips, hotels, talks, tears, laughs, and brainstorming sessions. Not many people get to be lifelong best friends, and business partners. Thanks for believing in this mission. We did it, bro!

Big thank you to Post Hill Press and all the staff who helped make this book a dream come true. I am so grateful for all the hard work and effort.

Thanks to the amazing and talented Wenonah Hoye, who wrote and contributed to this book. Thank you for putting up with me and talking to me for hours every week for several months. There are very few people in this world who truly know this story and I'm lucky to have partnered with you to bring the Project 615 journey to life on the page. Without your talent, creativity, passion, and knowledge, this book wouldn't exist. You're a prose pro. You helped translate this crazy foreign language and put it into words everyone can understand. You are helping inspire others to change the world. THANK YOU! I can't think of a better person to partner with on the writing of this book.

Thank you to my rock star assistant, Naomi Keel, who supported and coordinated so much to make this come alive. Thanks for your support and encouragement. Not only for this book, but for doing "work that matters" and helping change the world. You've ministered well to Project 615 and me. You've allowed my God-given talents to flourish. Not one day goes by that I'm not grateful for your servant heart you offer to everyone. You're a gift to all you speak with.

Thank you to Brentwood Baptist and friends for being our cheerleaders from the beginning. My dear friends: Scott Harris, Aaron Bryant, Keely Boggs, Roger Severino, Mignon Camp, and Mike Glenn. Thank you all for helping us becoming believers in God's calling. You all believed in a couple of kids in the audience, believed in our calling and poured gasoline on our fire. I've never seen people encourage and support the way all of you did since the beginning. THANK YOU!

To one of my lifelong brothers, Jonathan Harris. That little pizza party Bible study that I thought would be the nerdiest thing, turned into a lifelong friendship of some bad asses. You're an influencer. You're like a brother to me and I am grateful for how you always pursued our friendship. I'm honored to call you a friend. You challenge and encourage me in the best way. I always thought you would just forget about me early on but even when I felt down and out, you leaned in to grab a hand. To the rest of my band of brothers: Daniel Earls, DJ Farris, Phillip Vaughn, Thomas Summers, Drake White, Matt Owens, and Brandon England. All of you guys are great friends who supported and inspired me. Much love to you all!

To Bob Carlton and Ben Pitts, two good buddies who always encouraged us from day one. You didn't have to befriend these punk kids...but you did. I'm grateful for your friendship and encouragement over the years. Always love hearing "Go God!" from you both.

To all the Set Fee Pastors: Pastor Kirk Overstreet, Pastor Willie Dalgity, Pastor Marty Souter, Pastor Kenny Betzer and Pastor Tim Shaner: Thank you all for your leadership, friendship, and pastoral care from Set Free. You all taught me what grace and mercy truly looks like. You guys are my heroes! Also a big shout-out to David Mintzer. Love you, brother.

Thanks to my lifelong best friends: Jefferson Danner, Aaron Shanahan, Josh Michael, Coy Schrougham, Craig Woodfill, and Ryan Weiss.

To Uncle Keith: Thanks for always speaking optimism into my life, and for teaching and coaching me in sports. You have been a constant breath of encouragement. I am grateful to have you in my life. To Uncle Wayne: You are missed. Thanks for being a great uncle and coach, and for instilling a love for sports in my life. Both of you spoke great words of wisdom.

To my Southport crew: Great friends since day one. Matty J, Kit, Mike Z, Brent B, Huey man, Stevie Lee, Jay-Lo, Quin, Rit-Dawg. Thanks for all your friendship and laughs throughout the years. I am honored to grow up and continue to live life with you guys.

Last but not least: To my late grandparents. Robert & Janet Lunn and Ray & Audrey Evans. Thanks for molding me into the man I strive to be. May your legacy live on.

ABOUT THE AUTHOR

Derek Evans is president and co-founder of Project 615. In 2010, he launched his apparel company to do "work that matters" and utilize that platform to help change the world. Derek has helped hire fifty-four people recovering from homelessness, built an orphanage in Uganda, and raised over half a million dollars for various world-changing non-profit organizations. He lives with his wife in Nashville, TN. One hundred percent of the author's profits for this book will be donated to Room In The Inn.

For more information, visit madetochangetheworld.org. Contact Derek via email at Derek@madetochangetheworld.org.